The Lightness of Being You

Set free the joy, beauty and magic that live within you.

by Ann Ernst

With great love to Bob
You are my rock, my cheerleader and my joy,
And you make me laugh!
—A.E.

Copyright © 2010 by Ann Ernst

ALL RIGHTS RESERVED. No part of this book may
be reproduced or transmitted in any form by any means,
electronic or mechanical, including photocopying and
recording, or by any information storage and retrieval system,
except as may be expressly permitted in writing
from the publisher.

ISBN 10: 1451500521
ISBN 13: 9781451500523

The Lightness of Being You™

www.thelightnessofbeingyou.com

CreateSpace

Manufactured in the United States of America

Contents

INTRODUCTION 7

You, Wonderful You

Chapter 1: THE WHOLE PACKAGE 20

Chapter 2: THE BRIGHT VISION 32

Chapter 3: SNAPSHOT OF THE WHOLE PACKAGE 46

Chapter 4: 1st L: LOVE 64

Lightness

Chapter 5: LIGHT/DARK 76

Chapter 6: DRAGONS 101

Chapter 7: 2nd L: LIMIT 115

Chapter 8: 3rd L: LAUGH 130

Live it!

Chapter 9: YOUR LIGHT PATH 140

Chapter 10: 4th L: LIVE LIGHTNESS 160

NOTES 178

INTRODUCTION

Welcome to Lightness of Being!

Lightness of Being invites you to view yourself and your life from a new perspective and use what you see to live the life you intend. It means looking at your life and knowing you can control and direct its course.

In my work as a life and an executive coach, I've seen so many people who are locked in. They want to be in a different place, to have a different life, to work in another profession, to commit to another person. Yet they stay in place, unable to move — weighed down and unable to see the light, capture the light, or let their own internal light shine or even be turned on. Call this "creativity" or "brilliance" or "delight in living": it is the deepest core of their being which affects the context for living, working, playing and loving.

My hope is that as you read and work at Lightness of Being, you will gain a sense of yourself on the brink of a lighter and brighter life.

Over the course of my years of work with corporate leaders, managers, people in transition from one stage of life to another, I have come to hold strong personal convictions.

I should add that these convictions have also been born from personal experience and from being with those I love, both family and friends. They really are the standard bearers for lightness. Read them, post them and embrace them.

Convictions

The respect we have for ourselves determines our actions.

Self-image is not only how we see ourselves but the value we place on who we are.

How we treat others is a reflection of our core values.

We are empowered to act in our own best interest.

Lightness is possible for each of us.

Lightness of Being is a way of living your best life now. As you begin the process of exploring what lightness means for you and the changes you want to make, keep these reminders handy:

* ✳ You have extraordinary talents that are unexpressed.

* ✳ You will rise to the expectation you have of yourself.

* ✳ Personal growth demands time to reflect and to discern choices.

* ✳ Insight into your wants, needs, desires and behaviors can be a turning point, resulting in new and significant directions.

"Too many people die with their music still in them."
~ Oliver Wendell Holmes

Why I wrote Lightness of Being

It's simple: I decided that my own discovery of Lightness was a compelling experience, and I wanted to share it. The beliefs I live by make a profound difference in my life every day. I consciously choose to look on the bright side, to choose optimism, and to believe that I can limit what zaps the lightness from my life and makes me less than I want to be.

The best part for me is that I am now (at long last!) conscious of what gives me lightness and what takes it away. It is the speed with which I recognize and see or feel the signs of light-taking that helps me to quickly readjust. This is what I want for you.

In my coaching practice I meet people who are in positions and places that they don't want to be and who are doing things they don't want to be doing. They are stuck. I see people who, for any number of reasons, are controlled by circumstances that have kept them from moving forward in a well-lived life. I want to offer you the practical model that guides me. You might say that I'm the test of the practice of lightness. I want to share my experience with the hope that you will take what is helpful and integrate Lightness into your day-to-day patterns of living.

How to use this book

This book was made to delight, empower and illuminate the way to live your life fully right now. It includes tools and techniques, examples and exercises to move you along the path to lightness. I hope it will stimulate your thinking and give you the luxury of learning about you. Insight and awareness are its goals.

Here's how the book works: I share my observations and things I've learned from my own experiences and those of clients. You can make the information relevant to your situation by simply adjusting a situation, expanding a story, changing a gender. You can tailor the content to make the examples fit you. I share; you reflect.

The time you spend thinking, reflecting and clarifying is the best part, the really self-indulgent part, the pleasure part. I hope you will write down your observations and insights, because writing offers another dimension of understanding.

In some ways, this is a workbook, but don't feel pressured to fill in the spaces left for writing. They are merely there for you to use if you choose.

There are no rules!

You don't have to read The Lightness of Being You from cover to cover. You may decide to start with a topic of immediate interest or a section that interests you. For example, if you are feeling quite overwhelmed or burdened right now, you may decide to go directly to the Limit chapter in Part 2. If you have already spent quality time discovering who you are, you may want to begin with part 1, chapter 2, to create a vision for your future.

Consider finding a "lightness buddy" to read and work with. Challenge each other to be candid in your reflections and to be open to what surfaces for each of you. You can choose just how much or how little you wish to share with each other.

Most of all…enjoy!

Here is what I recommend:

Browse the book and get to know its layout and ideas.

Put it down and return to it when you are ready to move forward.

Start at the beginning and dive into each section as deeply as you want to.

Download extra worksheets from the Lightness website to make notes.

Keep adding to them as you gain new insights.

A preview of the process: Stepping stones

You are going to be reflecting on some BIG, TOUGH questions. Going forward, we'll break them open so that you can really get your arms around them. Consider them as stepping stones to discover lightness, what that means for you, and some ways to gain and sustain it. You may step on a certain stone only once, or you may go back to them several times. Do whatever you need to stay the path! The questions can be:

* Tough—ones you'd rather not hear the answers to.

* Uncomfortable—ones which can evoke buried feelings that you may not be ready to process.

* Surprising—ones which may lead to a host of additional questions that don't have easy answers. They may also give you ideas or highlight opportunities.

A small sampling:

What do you want? What do you really want?
What is your vision for how you want your life to be?
How do you see the next several years playing out?
How do you think you'll get there?
What holds you back?

Questions help you find the truth of who you really are. They are gifts from you to you!

The 4 L's of lightness, or let's keep it simple!

These are the tenets of lightness. They sound simple but are full of meaning. I'm going to build upon them as we go. You will notice that they have their own chapters. These were created from my own need to have a quick and easily remembered reference…my personal cheat sheet.

So I'm asking you, too, to remember these words and make them your own. The concepts behind them will become clear as we move forward. Briefly, here is a view of each of the L's.

Love and honor yourself, the whole package that is you!

Limit the Light-takers to make room for the Light-givers, the energizers.

Laugh and play more often; live in appreciation of life.

Live lightness every day.

> **Tweaking required…**
>
> To live by these 4 tenets of lightness, you may have to tweak how you think and act!

*"There is no way to tell people that they
are walking around shining like the sun."
~ Thomas Merton*

A new meaning for you

I find the idea of lightness life-changing. The word is rich in meaning and metaphor. In this book we embrace the word light and its meaning to describe this life path called Lightness of Being. You will build and hold your own definition. Here are just a few meanings to stir your thoughts and help to stimulate how you hear, see and feel what "Light" means to you:

✸ A young couple about to be engaged leaning over the glass counter of a fine jewelry store, where the salesperson is giving a scientific description of a diamond's "light" — its brilliance, clarity and color.

✸ A museum visitor gazing in awe at a series of Monet's "Haystack" painting while listening to an audio guide tell how Monet painted at different times of day to capture just the right slant of light on his subject.

✸ A wine lover swirling a glass of claret to see its "light"

✸ A musician interpreting a composer's instruction to play "sprightly and lightly."

Light can describe a color but also an idea that suddenly sparks in your brain and provides information or understanding. We say, "I finally saw the light!" A "light shining in the darkness" can mean spiritual awareness. We know a light can ignite and set us on fire, both figuratively and literally.

We can be filled with light. We can glow seeing an old friend or while telling a great story.

Consider "light" as a quality of having little weight; as an ease or quickness of movement; as agility. It is buoyancy, a feeling that bubbles up and brings a smile to your lips. A dictionary definition will give you "ease or cheerfulness in manner or style" and "freedom from worry or trouble."

Lightness of Being

It is the illumination and radiance inside you.

It is your enlightened self, in touch with the weights you carry.

Limit or eliminate what weighs you down and you will feel more agile.

It can set you on fire with passion for life.

We embrace all these rich meanings of "light."

Lightness is what you let into your being, your soul, your eyes, and it says, "I am unique. I am worthy of respect. I am full of vitality. I am in control."

A lightness of being primer

Lightness is a guide for living your life.

It is a way of life that commands both optimism and realism.

Lightness lifts weights to strengthen your inner core.

Lightness gives control and courage new respect.

It is the lens through which you see your life and view it with deep pleasure.

It energizes and releases creativity.

It invites you to be playful.

Lightness is comfort and joy.

18

You, Wonderful You

CHAPTER 1

The Whole Package

Your first step is to learn, to discover and to be aware of the whole wonderful package that is YOU. While you're at it, learn about the "imp" inside you. Before you start poking around, let me introduce the Imp.

Love, Limit, Laugh, Live Lightness

Each of us has a playful side: mischievous, spontaneous, and highly creative. Our day-to-day rational selves don't give that impish side of our personality much attention. I know that if we did we would be astounded by how likable, intelligent and imaginative he or she is! The Imp has the capacity to unearth surprises and bring to light aspects of our personality that might open new doors. Give the Imp permission to disrupt your conventional thinking as you get to know yourself in this next activity.

"If you obey all the rules, you miss all the fun."
~ Katharine Hepburn

Self awareness is more than being aware that you are alive and able to feel. It is insight into your life experiences, your feelings, behaviors, beliefs and how they shape you and make you unique. It is an appreciation of the complexity of your personality that makes you different from anyone else who ever lived.

The deeper the knowledge we have about what makes us tick, the more certain we are about what drags us down and undermines our best efforts to be fully alive. We need to be awake and alert, watchful and vigilant to signs and signals hat tell us when we're wandering off into troublesome territory.

Self awareness is not the same as "navel gazing" or being self absorbed. It is a healthy regard for the goodness, the brilliance and infinite potential of who we are and what we can become. It is about making the connection to who we are becoming.

Our identity can be formed by other people: many of whom can be critical, judgmental or disapproving. But what is essential to perceiving ourselves is our own centering, our own values and our intimate understanding of who we are at the core of our being.

When we are comfortable in our own skin, we are confident, grounded, and open to hearing and observing. We can listen to our critics, as well as our supporters, without being thrown off center or teased away from our goals. We honor ourselves.

"No one can make you feel inferior without your consent."
~ Eleanor Roosevelt

Your deeply held values…

Once you get in touch with the values that you hold for yourself, those values that guide your life and are obvious to all who truly know you, you are able to continually reinforce the habit of honoring yourself.

All your action and behaviors match those values. You are true to who you are deep down inside. You don't rely on others to define you.

So many of us have built up habits of doing what is expected of us rather than being comfortable and accepting of who we really are. We may have been socialized as children to please, to conform to standards that don't fit us as adults. Influences of family and culture can shape us, but to honor ourselves we live by our own values. Honoring yourself is not selfish. It's about care and wholeness.

But first, you must identify what those values are for you, and what they mean to you. Your values come from you, not from any proscribed list. You may have a value that has the same name as someone else's, but the meanings for each of you may be different.

> **Embrace your values**
>
> Open your heart and just identify them.
>
> Respect them, don't judge them.
>
> When you honor your values, you honor yourself.
>
> You owe it to you!

Take a value such as financial security:

For Joe, it means being frugal, never having any credit cards and saving X% every month.

For Amy, it means having the money to buy whatever she wants, a feeling of independence and $Y in net worth.

You get the drift!

During coaching sessions, my clients identify and really get in touch with their values. They didn't arrive at them in one single moment or sitting. Each of them started a list, expanded it, clarified each point and finally said, "This is my list." Often the next step is to identify the top three to five values. Think of them as absolutes, as essential to your well-being as water and sleep.

Here are some that have surfaced for others during the course of coaching.

"Honesty… is number one for me. I get completely out of sorts if this need is not met. I cannot be in any sort of relationship without it. I would feel cheated. I actually left my last job because my boss was not honest about anything that mattered."
Helen T., MA

"Beauty is so critical to my fulfillment. For me this means being able to get up in the morning and see a lovely flower or put my feet down on a beautifully designed, brightly colored rug. Those spots of beauty just fill my soul. Beauty is closely related to my value around art and creativity."
Carl W., CT

"Ever since I can remember, I have sought independence. To me, it means the ability to make my own decisions and stand on my own two feet. It is coupled with my strong need for financial security, which helps me to be independent."
Sandy P., CA

Summer and stepping stones to lightness

Last summer on Cape Cod, Sarah set aside time to consider some life changes. She answered some questions that had been nagging her for several years.

Since she was very young, Sarah had wanted to be an elementary school teacher. She loved helping young children learn about insects and nature. Nothing buoyed her spirits more than watching the delight of children as they discovered new things. She basked in the glow of their shining eyes. In college, she majored in science education. She also studied computer science, based on the advice of her academic advisor, because the job market was wooing bright students interested in a growth career and a competitive salary. After years of just making ends meet, the idea of a fat paycheck was very appealing. Upon graduation, Sarah accepted a programmer trainee position with a large international bank.

After nine years of progressing from programmer to data architect, she was feeling unfulfilled, with a deep longing that was not satisfied. Sarah knew her job dissatisfaction would only grow more intense if she remained in a technology career. In her dreams she could see children with grubby fingers digging for sand worms.

Sarah's soul-searching about what she really wanted and her courage to go for it resulted in her switch from technology to elementary education. Her decision to honor what she really wanted was slow to come. She sacrificed financially but felt she was finally in touch with, as she put it, the "real Sarah."

Thumbs up to this young woman!

IMP Wisdom!

Show some respect for your values.

They are as unique and priceless as you are.

Live according to them and enjoy a fulfilling life!

Think about your values and take notes

You are identifying your values so that you will understand what you need to be fulfilled. It will help you to understand why you are dissatisfied in certain areas of your life. Don't be concerned about creating your be-all and end-all list. Just get started. You will revisit and refine as you move through the book.

Find a quiet place, put your feet up, close your eyes and think about a special moment that was full of joy or deep pleasure and see what surfaces. Go into it and truly experience what you felt at that moment.

What was meaningful to me about this special moment?

_____

_____

_____

_____

_____

_____

_____

_____

My values
Keep going. You are on a roll!

These questions will help:

What do I stand for?
What do I need in order to truly be who I am?
What is vital to me?
What can't I live without?
What is present when I am at my best?

_____

_____

_____

_____

_____

_____

_____

_____

Take action!

Select one of your top five values and purposefully honor it over the next two weeks.

1. Fully embrace it and what it means to you.

2. Insert it into your conversations.

3. Make choices based on it.

4. Give yourself "high fives."

5. Record your experience as you wish:
   Tell your buddy,
   Place a note on the fridge,
   Journal about it...you get the idea!

CHAPTER 2

Your Bright Vision

Let the excitement begin...
You are going to envision what you want
for yourself, for your life!

Turning to lightness

You may have come to Lightness of Being out of a need to move from one place to another. You want to move toward what you want and need to be and do. Change, growth, unrealized potential, stress and crisis are strong motivators for action. Choice and change require learning and increased self-awareness. You are forming your own vision of a future in which you are honored and authentic — true to the person you are deep down inside.

You need to be clear about what it is you are turning away from as well as what you are turning toward. It may be that you have come to a turning point in your life and that you are very ready for change.

"To live is to choose.
But to choose well, you must know
who you are and what you stand
for, where you want to go and why
you want to get there."
~ Kofi Annan

You may be ready to turn away from:

Dissatisfaction:
There is something that is causing disquiet with one or more of the pieces of your life and you know it is not good. It is a nagging concern that demands attention. It is a discontent in spite of your best efforts to endure in a situation that makes you uncomfortable or worse.

A hollow feeling that signals a deep unrest:
This may feel like emptiness. A passion is ignored; a value is not honored. This unmet need is no longer acceptable to you. You may be trying to live up to another's expectations with a halfhearted effort. This hollowness leaves you feeling unfulfilled.

The present routine:
Maybe you are hoping that a fresh start will recapture your optimism and bring the future into sharp focus. The past did not suit you. You see new challenges, a change of venue and pace; nurturing relationships on a horizon you intend to create for yourself, one suited to your strengths and preferences. The current routine drains your energy, and you feel listless.

Consider...

It may be that you just want to be in a place that is better and lighter for you!

What would my best life look like?

It doesn't matter which area of your life you want to be different, better or lighter. Your vision applies to your whole life…it's the essence of you. For some of you, the vision is well known; you are certain of your purpose in life. You have been thinking, dreaming and talking about it for a long time. It has depth and breadth for you, and lots of details. But you never got around to it!

Life got in the way, it just didn't seem feasible, and it looked too big, too risky, too radical, too selfish and too different.

For many of you, the vision is something that is deep down inside you and exists through a deep inner knowing. It must be teased out through reflection and time. The time you have already spent in articulating your values is part of the teasing and the wonder of self-discovery. There is true fulfillment and pleasure just in the learning and acknowledgement of what you want for your life.

You may be closer than you think!

"There is nothing like a dream to create the future."
~ Victor Hugo

In my coaching, I have often encountered people who say they haven't a clue about what they truly want, what their passion in life is. They believe that it doesn't exist for them or that it must be some grandiose thing. Others know their passion and purpose with an unwavering certitude. For one friend of mine, the passion is "giving back." It is simple in its statement but profound in what it means to her, how it colors her world and how it fills her up.

Paula's passion

"I want to have a richer life, more balance, serenity, doing the things I love and having some truly fulfilling relationships with kindred spirits. Sometimes I dream of starting a community garden and being surrounded by other enthusiastic gardeners, preparing wonderful meals with just-picked vegetables. I can't do it now; I really need to wait until my children are out of the nest."
—Paula R. Quebec, Canada

If Paula just shared her vision and her longings with you,

What questions would you ask her?

What advice would you give her?

Picture a mountain cabin...

As many of us do, Sam spent his days and the majority of his time at work. His job paid well and he liked his coworkers and boss. Once a year, Sam and his family took a vacation to the mountains. There he spent time on the lake, reading, taking long walks with his wife and just being. It was pleasant, and the time spent fishing with his sons was truly joyful. They would have grand chats and feel very close. There was laughter in the air and a feeling that life was good.

During one of these sojourns at the mountain cabin, Sam began reflecting on his life and seeing a vision of what he truly wanted. For a long time, he had felt a bit detached from his boys and out of touch with nature. At the cabin, he found moments that made his heart sing and realized that was a seldom felt experience back in the real world. One thing that he was sure of was that he loved his wife and kids and was always happy being with them.

Sam longed for more peace, more laughter, more communing with nature. When he closed his eyes and reflected on what he truly wanted for his life, this is what surfaced: It would be filled with special moments with his children and wife, in a special place that was close to nature. He would grow and learn as a person and also teach his children things. He would interact with other people, but also have alone time to nurture his soul. He would set his own pace and have greater control over his destiny. He would live simply, have a strong spiritual life and feel an abundance of love all around him.

As Sam delved more deeply into the vision, he saw himself

making a living as an entrepreneur watching over his own enterprise rather than as an employee working a routine job. He saw the enterprise as providing not only a living but time for his family and beloved pursuits.

He had always dreamed of owning a sort of Bait and Tackle, outdoor adventure business in a community that he would feel part of, where he would be able to bond with the nature around him.

Soon the vision became even more defined. Sam pictured living on a few acres near a mountain lake and getting up every day to a view of the water, often having his morning coffee on the deck. A little later, he would unlock the door to his store and enjoy helping and interacting with other nature enthusiasts.

He saw his sons and wife as a part of the business, all of them spending quality, fun-filled time together each day. He saw the chance to get back in touch with his own personal growth and spirituality and to strengthen his bonds with his wife and children. He liked that it didn't seem easy and it involved some risk. He envisioned what choices he would have and what rewards were possible!

Sam felt energized by this vision of his life. He was clearly aware of how it made his heart sing, that he felt

Sam is on his way

He has clearly articulated his vision.

He is very aware of what gives him light.

He is in touch with his core.

He is living lightness.

buoyed up and simply more alive. He felt lighter and brighter just picturing the vision in his mind.

Stay tuned for Sam's light path!
(CHAPTER 9)

What about you?

Perhaps, you want to make a graceful shift from employment to retirement, or you want to step into a career that fits your personality better. You may want to change a personal relationship that is making you unhappy into one that is satisfying. You may want to live in a place that is "more you." The possibilities are endless and unique to each person.

You took the first step by forming a clear picture of who you are, what you need and who you are becoming. Once you know that, you can build upon it with measures of lightness.

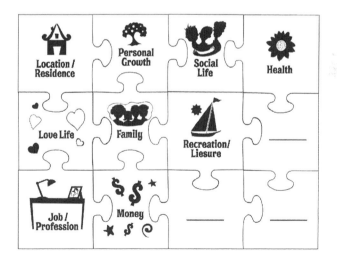

Create a vision of the life you want

So where are we going with this? You are going to set about "painting" a bright vision for your life. Let the various compartments of your life, your passions, values, strengths and preferences, enter into it.

The purpose of the following exercise is to picture yourself in the future as a new creation —the one you want to be. There will not be a quiz. This is just for you, and it should be fun. You will be using a meditation; enjoy where it takes you. Your imagination will lead the way. Allow the meditation to expand in your mind.

Find a quiet place where you will not be interrupted for 15 minutes. Get comfortable, read the meditation, close your eyes and breathe easily. Relax your muscles. Then simply bask in what surfaces. Take the time to really enjoy this.

(Note: there are other meditations available for download from www.thelightnessofbeingyou.com)

Take the time

Think from your heart.

Be in tune with your senses.

Be in tune with your intuition.

Fill in the details of the landscape of your life.

A garden of delight

You lift the latch of the gate. It swings in and you walk into a secluded garden. It is quiet, with only the sounds of birds in the distance. You find a bench in a shady spot under a spreading tree. Your view is filled with lush greenery, flowering garden beds and fragrant shrubs. You sit and dream with the warm sun on your back. You move forward five years into the future and spend time with your future self. You begin to sink into your dream and allow yourself to be in it completely...

Revel in the dream

Where were you? What was the setting like?

What were you doing?

What was thrilling about it?

How did you feel, physically and emotionally?

Were there colors that were brighter or more prevalent?

Who else was there with you?

IMP Wisdom!

Your vision evokes such pleasure.

It is just so right for you.

Embrace the magic and pleasure of your vision.

Savor it, smell, taste, feel and chew on it.

Then live it!!!

Building blocks for your vision

Get in touch with your thoughts and feelings and jot down your answers. Take a light approach and enjoy what shows up.

1. What do you want to turn away from?

2. What do you want to get rid of, adjust, rearrange or change?

3. What do you want to turn toward?

4. What do you want? What do you want for your life?

5. What's really important to you?

6. What makes your heart sing?

7. What are you doing when you're at your best?

8. Are there pieces missing from the fullness of your life?

9. What are you yearning for, longing to have in your life? What are you willing to do or to risk to have it?

10. What have you always dreamed of doing with your life?

    What thrills you about what you've always dreamed of?

    What's gotten in the way of doing it?

11. How close are you now to what you want for you?

12. What one thing can you do today to begin living your vision?

Take action!

Five brilliant things you can do to make the vision a part of you:

1. Keep a small notebook with you at all times and write down more and more details about your vision

2. Put a vision board somewhere prominent in your home and keep adding to and refining it.

3. Paint or draw what you want for your life.

4. Describe it to a trusted friend and ask him/her to be curious about it.

5. Fast forward five years from now and write your bio.

CHAPTER 3

Snapshot of the Whole Package

You know so much more about what is essential to your well-being. Now it's time to take your snapshot at this wondrous point in your life. This picture will capture where you are in your life and how you look at this moment; the outer reflection of you is also meaningful. What's the whole package that is you now and how did you arrive at this moment? What supports your best life, and what might be taking from it?

I suggest that you create a personal report describing where you are right now. You will be pleased by some of the things you see, saddened by and possibly even angered by some. Go with what you see. It will spur you on to take action.

The big goal of this chapter is for you to gauge how close you are to living life the way you want and what sorts of things you are willing to do or to give up to have the life you want. Poke around; see what's there now; do the difficult thinking. Out of this reflection, possibilities or opportunities may emerge. Go with the flow and see what surfaces. After all, you are making some discoveries about a truly fascinating person… YOU!!

You are so worth it!!

The Snapshot

It is important to know where you are right now,

to see what you are becoming

as you take a stand for what you want and what you need.

Life's a circus!

Below are some stories I've heard from clients. Can you relate to any of them? Consider using a circus moniker as they have, to describe where you are right now when you create your personal report.

I'm mad as hell! My job was cut. I got no severance package and
I'm 41 years old.
—Caged Lion

Today I feel balanced. I think I'm doing a good job keeping things
going at home. I'd rate my performance high. I feel centered,
proud of what I've accomplished, and generally optimistic about
the future.
—Ringmaster

My boss says "Jump" and I say "How high?" I know the tricks of
how to please by now but I don't like myself.
—Trained Dog

I'm alone, but I'm definitely a risk-taker. If an opportunity presents itself, I grab it. I'll figure things out along the way, as I go along. I've always been brave when it comes to taking a chance. The risk pays off most of the time. If it doesn't, I start over. If I have regrets, they don't last long.
—*High Wire Artist*

I put up a good front because of my kids. But I need out. I'm trapped. I never bargained for this life. Really, I'm dead inside.
—*Sad Clown*

I love this title! Cannon fodder speaks to me. Half the time I feel like I'm set up to fail. I get the flak when it's not me who screws up.
—*Man in a Cannon*

How did I get to here?

You find yourself here, now, with a life you may or may not have fully intended. What brought you here? How did you get to where you are right now? Use the items below to help you think about what shaped your present life. You may want to go to the end of the chapter and make some notes on your personal report.

✴ Conscious decisions or no decisions

✴ Choice of partner, spouse, friends

✴ Family expectations

✴ Help or lack of help along the way

✴ Opportunities seized or neglected

✴ Mistakes or excellent choices

✴ Good decisions and some not so good

✴ Influences that gave shape to your life

Snapshot: The parts and heart of you

Let's take a look at the many parts of your life. Think of it as a puzzle, with all of the pieces conjoining and meeting in different ways. Some fit snugly together and other pieces don't.
Let's explore and see what's what.

Your life is made up of several pieces or areas.
You give them time, energy and attention in varying degrees.
They support and reinforce one another...or not.
What happens in one area can have either a positive or negative impact on another area of your life.

This a pretty good list of them:
Location/Residence, Love Life, Job/Profession, Family, Social Life, Health, Recreation/Leisure,
Money, Personal Growth

You will be taking a look at each piece, assessing your satisfaction level, and also examining how in or out of balance your life is.

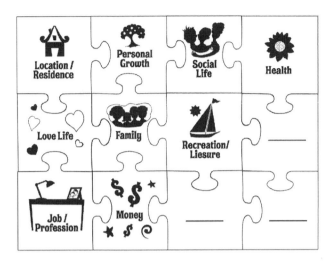

Are there any other pieces you would add? Feel free to add or change a piece...after all, it is your life!

The meanings are yours. For example, Location/Residence could mean anything from your actual abode to your neighborhood, state, region or country. It could have nuances regarding culture, environment, and topography; urban vs. country. You get it...make each piece meaningful for you.

Identify your satisfaction level for each piece:
Very High (V), High (H), Medium (M), Low (L), Abysmal (A)

This is not scientific, just an appraisal from your wisest self.

Passions and yearnings

"Only passions, great passions, can elevate the soul to great things."
~Denis Diderot

So often, you hear people talk about wanting to do something different. The conversation goes something like this: "For as long as I can remember, I've wanted to have a farm, be self-sustaining and be able to look out every morning at my land and crops. But it would be impossible. I have too many responsibilities, and my wife and kids hate the idea." Then there are those who talk about wanting to give up a very stressful yet lucrative career in order to become a [fill in the blank].

Sometimes these longings go unfulfilled because the person cannot see what the true longing is, or they cannot see beyond the obstacles or their own personal dragons. It may be that they have not clearly identified the true passion.

You have certain passions that drive and ignite you.
You may or may not give them time, energy or attention.
This is your time to "speak out" about them and say all that they represent for you.

How easy is it to recognize a passion, your own or someone else's? Perhaps, you cannot stop talking about it or there is evidence of it in your living space. For some, it is the unmentioned or obviously avoided. For some, it is waiting to be discovered.

For David, it is to be a crusader and to bring about social change. For Martha, it is art...you see it in her home, you hear it in her references and you know it by her activities. For Stephanie, it is photography; she has had a camera attached to her since her teen years. For Mary Ann and for Beth, it is creating fine meals and desserts and sharing them with those they love. For Jerry, it is birding, and he has made a successful business of his passion.

A great passion may be:

A cause

A life's work

A profession

A hobby

A pleasant pursuit

A sport

A style of living

When considering what your passion might be, do not be afraid to say what might sound wild and crazy, or the deep down yearning you truly feel. After all these are your passions and your longings.

What I have also observed is that passions and longings are bundled with deeply held values.
I can't be with...

54

You now have quite a bit of information about you. But wait, there's more before your snapshot is complete! Here is what you still need to do. Identify what you can't tolerate. Sometimes what you cannot tolerate are simple things that you don't get around to dealing with, and sometimes they are situations that are huge and complex.

Identifying the intolerable may help you articulate other hidden thoughts and feelings.

"One is responsible for one's own life.
Passivity provides no protection."
~ Madeleine Kunin

Here are some "can't be with's" I've heard from my coaching clients:

"Every morning when I walk downstairs, the sight of that wallpaper in the hallway makes me cringe.
I hate it; it is so ugly."
Carolyn G, CT

"Sunday nights are becoming unbearable. I lay awake half the night dreading the fact that I have to go into work Monday morning to a job that is becoming intolerable.
I just don't know if I can handle it another day."
Tom K., Switzerland

"I thought that retiring and moving to Arizona would be bliss. Instead it is a nightmare. I honestly don't know if it is retirement, Arizona or 24/7 with my husband that is making me feel so dissatisfied.
Something has got to change!"
Jane Z., AZ

"Joe and I have been friends since high school and I used to enjoy spending time with him. However, the past several times we've been together, he had too much to drink and became very argumentative, loud and obnoxious. I was a wreck at the end of the evening; our friendship is in jeopardy."
Al B., FL

It bubbles up

As you have probably figured out by now, this is serious work you are doing on your own behalf. But we are trying to keep it light with a bit of whimsy. Stay in touch with your inner Imp, tap into the wisdom and break the bonds that sometimes confine your thinking.

It is of great benefit to look at life from different sides. It has been my experience that many of you will have more success identifying what you truly want after you have thought through what you cannot stand or cannot be with.

After having a good look at yourself, you can make some decisions about where you want to be and what you need to do. You will know what's really working well for you and what you want to change to live the life you want. In the exercises that follow, take a light approach. Be the fish blowing bubbles and see what bubbles up.

.

IMP Wisdom!

You know exactly where you are right now.

You are in touch with what's important to you.

You have the power, the right and the stuff to create your best life!

My personal puzzle

Reflect on the satisfaction levels you identified for the various pieces of your life.

1. Consider the pieces that you must change for your life to be infinitely more satisfying.
    * What do you want to pay special attention to?

    * What is causing the most pain?

    * What presents a new opportunity?

2. Now prioritize. What are your number 1 and 2 priorities?

3. What changes that will have to be made?
   What changes will you commit to making?

The art of discovery…it's all about light

1. What turns the Light ON for you?

2. What turns the Light OFF for you?

3. What releases your Imp — that playful side that's fun to be with?

4. What MUST you have? It could be something you need all the time or just periodically.

Something has got to change

Here are some can't be with questions. Your thoughtful answers provide perspective on what you're willing to change.

1. What can't you live with another day?

2. What keeps you awake at night?

3. What's the one thing you could fix that would make your life/situation better and lighter?

Passions plus…

Pinpoint your longings, passions, always wanted to's or to have's.

Go to a favorite place or room and get comfortable. This is going to be a conversation with you about what you want. Talk to yourself—yes, out loud—and say what's on your mind. Perhaps it has been there for a long time, or perhaps it just hit you. Write it down. Include as much detail as possible.

Take action!

4 things you can do right now to be lighter

1. Pick a periodic "must have" and have it today!
   a. (Examples: a concert, once-a-season-lobster-in-Maine, a walk in the woods, alone time)

2. Begin to forge a plan for the "can't be with" and take the first step. (Example: Caroline actually started scraping the wallpaper off the wall and forced her plan into action.)

3. Do something by tomorrow to ratchet up your satisfaction level with one piece of your life.

4. Start writing your Personal Report

CHAPTER 4

The 1st L: LOVE

We have all heard from the self-help gurus that we must first of all love ourselves. Sometimes that's a tall order, and it sounds so self-absorbed, self-centered…you know what I mean. So let's be really clear about this 1st L: LOVE.

Here is the simple truth: The more you love yourself, the more you will be able to love others. Looking at yourself through loving eyes makes it more possible for you to look at others through loving, benevolent eyes.

"To love oneself is the beginning of a lifelong romance."
~ Oscar Wilde

Let's get something straight...

When I work with clients who love and honor themselves, I see them moving through life on a fulfilling, light-filled path. Loving yourself is a commitment that you make, and it is an act of courage, by you and for you.

Leading a fulfilling life is not about perfection...far from it. It is an authentic way to live, with full self-knowledge, warts and all. There are bumps in every road, and often they are great waker-uppers. It is about standing up for yourself, for the whole wonderful and unique package that is you. It is living life in concert with your values.

Sometimes you will veer from your chosen path, and when the love and awareness of self are strong, you'll get back on. It may mean retracing a few steps, but so what?

Love

Your self: body, mind and spirit.

Your values.

Your wants and needs.

Your priorities.

Your passions.

Your pursuits.

Your limitations.

65

Introducing the Love Imp!!

Allow the love side of your Imp to encourage you to fully embrace the 1st L:

Love
**Love and honor yourself,
the whole magnificent package that is you!**

Appreciate and accept who are.
Affirm your unlimited potential.
Be clear about the life you want.
Know what gives you Light.
Know what makes your heart sing.
Identify what's holding you back.
Be courageous in honor of yourself.

I love to…

One of the most critical things in achieving lightness is ever-increasing self-knowledge. We're not talking about hours and hours spent thinking about it, but rather being in tune to what your body, your mind, your heart and your intuition are telling you. They speak loudly. Just get used to listening.

What are you good at? What do you simply LOVE to do? What is your passion? What can't you stand doing? When does the time seem to fly? What do you enjoy and persist in doing (even though you may not be great at it)? Where are you when you're at your best? When are you humming to yourself?

One man's passion

I have been working with Tony, the third-generation owner of a construction company, for several years. We have been working on his exit plan and the eventual takeover of the company by his son, Michael. Michael puts in long, labor-intensive hours and spends time in the evenings learning about the business side of the company. Tony has huge passion for his business and feels great personal satisfaction whenever he sees a building that his company has constructed. He truly loves what he does, and he's good at it.

Michael is making an all-out effort to learn the business, to do the day-to-day work and to make his dad proud. But Tony is distressed by Michael's lack of passion for the business and the fact that he acts as if it is "just a job." Truth be told, Michael is unhappy because he doesn't believe that he has what it takes to run the business successfully. He doesn't love the work, and he has been experiencing some signs of a stomach ulcer.

Michael is most himself when the work week is over. He spends hours at the potter's wheel creating beautiful and unique objects and also working in his garden. This is when he comes alive. Friends and family love receiving one of his glazed pots or a basket of fresh-picked squash. Every once in a while, a friend will say, "You should open a little shop and sell your pottery. People would be lining up to buy it!" He may be doing work on the weekend, but it feels more like play to Michael. He is truly blissful and shines with a creative glow when he is doing what he loves.

Help Michael to live a light-filled life...

What do you think? Is Michael truly in touch with what he loves? Is he honoring himself?

What kind of courage would it take for Michael to stand up for his best life?

What would you do next if you were Michael?

Discover what you love and how you love to be

From a positive place deep within yourself, discover what you really love. This can encompass your work, your play, or all facets of your life. The idea is to let the thoughts flow, not to box in your thinking. For those of you who looked at your puzzle and were less than thrilled with your job/profession, think about that piece of your life. Remember that each piece bumps up against the other pieces and has an impact on every other piece, and the whole.

One thing I always encourage people to do is to consider the aspects of your life that are really fulfilling right now as well as the ones that aren't. Looking at the whole range can give you some bright ideas for the unsatisfying areas of your life. Focusing on what is fulfilling will help you to get in touch with what makes your heart sing, with what makes the time fly, and with what gives you energy and light.

You may already be doing the thing or things you love, or you may have only just discovered what they are. You may not be the world's greatest at whatever it is you love, but that's no problem. If you love to do it, it will energize

Focus on the Fulfilling

Get in touch with:

What makes your heart sing.

What makes time fly.

What gives you energy and light.

What brings a smile to your face and to your whole being.

you, and it will be worth your time and effort. Remember, it's not just about what you're doing but how you are when you're doing it.

It may be something you do to relax…something as simple as listening to a fine piece of music and feeling consumed and warm and effervescent. It may be teaching kindergarten and seeing the amazement in a student's eyes when she reads for the first time. This amazement fills the teacher with delight and joy as well.

I recently met a marketing professional who talked about loving his work. He had a law degree but gave up the practice of law to work in marketing. What was most noticeable was the pride that he exhibited when talking about his work. His chest was puffed out and he had a smile of well-being on his face.

What do you love to do? What are you really good at? What are you meant to do? What do you value doing? What gives you great satisfaction? What gives you that wonderful heartfelt buoyancy?

Part of discovering what you love to do is about how you love to be. (In the next section, when you reflect on lightness vs. darkness, you will get a better sense of this.) For example, do you love to be filled with excitement, ready to take on the world, creative, open to adventure? This may be just a sampling of the way you are when you do what you love. Also imagine the converse…when you do what you don't love.

So, how do you love to be? Busier than a one-armed paper-hanger, challenged, relaxed, structured, unstructured, having everything under control…?

> "Seek out that which makes you feel most deeply and vitally alive…the inner voice which says, 'This is the real me'."
> ~ William James

Honest answers will help propel you on your light path.

IMP Wisdom!

Love

Love yourself.

Love what you do.

Love what you are being.

Look in the mirror and SMILE!

Focus on the fulfilling

This is the time to be very aware of what you love and to acknowledge what fulfills you. Think broadly and stay focused!

1. What have you done in the past month that makes your heart sing?

2. When you think about it, how do you feel: Physically, emotionally, and intellectually?

3. What other things give you a similar feeling, but you haven't done any of them in ages? What's kept you from them?

4. Get creative. How can you go about fitting the fulfilling into your life?

Take action

4 things you can do right away to show some love:

1. Give an Imp report to a close friend.

2. Pick a value of the week and see how well you're able to honor it.

3. Every morning (preferably after you've pushed the snooze button) when you are enjoying a few more minutes in bed: Think of 10 things that you really love about yourself.

4. Do something you know you love to do.

Lightness

CHAPTER 5

Light/Dark

The idea for this concept began one sunny day when I had an epiphany that I decided to call Lightness of Being. For months, a too-full calendar, work, chores, extra weight and other things had held me down. I felt overwhelmed and trapped. Then I looked out my window and saw a beautiful goldfinch sitting on a branch that was gently swaying in the breeze. He was bathed by the sun and looked so at one with his world.

All of a sudden, I got up from my desk and said, "I want to feel light like that beautiful bird, and to keep that joyous, almost bubbly feeling I had when I spotted him." I could only describe it as Lightness of Being.

So what did this mean to me? What did I do about it? First I cleared my calendar. Next I took a large piece of paper and wrote "Lightness of Being" on it, with lots of colors and a picture of the sun, and hung it on the wall. What I found was that I could call up the lightness by just taking a deep breath, saying lightness, and summoning up the bubbly feeling. It is a palpable, sensory, "picture-able" feeling, and it sustains me… my hope for you is that it will sustain you also.

A few months later, I decided to share this concept with others. You are now holding the product of my sharing!! May it lead you to joy and renewed energy and to living lightness.

"Deep in their roots, all
flowers keep the light."
—Theodore Roethke

Light: The energizer

Light is the sun, bright as it can be. For me, it is also a positive, self-affirming confidence. If we are living life the best we can, there's a good chance that all will be right with our world. It doesn't mean we are perfect or that our lives are perfect. It just means we're moving around in a lighter place. Light is winning. It is life-sustaining. It is energizing. It is a source of power.

Light as a source of power gives us hope and helps us in our darkest hours. I think of these words: "After the darkest hour of defeat comes the golden dawn of the morning." Light brings us calmness. It is the power of "positivity" and possibilities. For many of us, light is where our passion is. It is what we're passionate about. And there's a reality here. It's not what I call "foo-foo dust." It is not simply, "If I think in a positive way, everything will be OK." It's more about thinking positively to keep us energized but also accepting reality. Think about the Serenity Prayer. What derails us, what eclipses or takes away our light and turns our light off, are fear and negativity. I'm sure you have your own energizer that you turn to when things seem to be falling apart.

We are familiar with the fact that light illuminates — whether it's the glow from a reading lamp or the beam of a battery-operated flashlight. Light helps us see. Think of a spotlight on a theater stage, the beacon of a lighthouse, or the tiny flame of a match that ignites a campfire in a dark forest.

Here, as we speak of Lightness of Being, we expand and extend the concept with another meaning. Light is both the absence of weight, and a sense of freedom. But light also is energy and clear vision. It is only when we have the experience of lightness of mind and spirit that we are free, energized, refreshed, and open to seeing new possibilities.

On a recent trip...

I was driving through Maine and stopped at a rest area to walk my dog. A truck driver struck up a conversation with me. He was eager to talk. He was going for a drug test, and his anxiety was palpable. He had no reason to fear the outcome, but he was filled with fear and "what ifs." I could tell he was wound up tight and in a dark place. He could not see beyond the possibility of a bad outcome. I think he was trying to avoid his bad feelings by talking to me.

It occurred to me that this casual meeting was an example of what light means. One of the qualities of true lightness is not letting imagined or irrational fears overtake you.

Calmness and clarity

Light also brings calmness and serenity, and if we think of light as bringing us clarity, that's what's really going to help us. That clarity will allow creativity in. When you think about clarity, picture and try to feel a beautiful sunny day, a great night's sleep, a trembling iris, an animal at play, anything that gave you lightness and took you into a light moment.

When we consider light, we need to look at it holistically. Consider your physical, spiritual, and intellectual selves. Where are you in lightness with them?

*"Count your smiles instead of your tears;
count your courage instead of your fears."*
—Anonymous

Your physical self

So many of us have dealt with the ups and downs of dieting, and we get weighed down both by the extra pounds and by the pressure to shed them. For some, it's about health; for others it's self-image. "I felt so good when I exercised! But now I don't have time for it." Others may have a health issue that they're ignoring because there just isn't enough time in the day to go to the doctor!

Reflect on the state of your physical self; decide whether each question gets a 👍 or a 👎.

* Are you weighed down by inches, pounds or aches and pains?

* Are you out of shape?

* Do you have enough stamina to play with your children or to take a hike with your partner?

* Did you stop doing something that you love to do because you are not feeling up to par?

* Do you love your body?

So where are you now? Take some time to reflect on how well your physical self is serving your lightness. What did you discover? You may want to take a moment to jot down some notes.

Your spiritual self

Spirituality is a different thing for each person. It is unlike our physicality, with which we can all identify. The spiritual is highly personal, inner and deep. And I'm not talking about religion—although it may mean that for you. For some people it's just looking out at a tree or a star and feeling the awesomeness of the universe. Look and be in touch with your inner feelings, your soul, and your center.

Reflect on the state of your spiritual self; decide whether each question gets a 👍 or a 👎.

* Is there a sacred place inside you where you can go and feel peace?

* Are you in touch with your spiritual dimension?

* Do you have an understanding of what spirituality is for you?

* Were you once in touch with your inner and deep self?

So where are you now? Take some time to reflect on how well your spiritual self is serving your lightness. What did you discover? You may want to take a moment to jot down some notes.

Your intellectual self

Just as your body requires some discipline and exercise, so does your mind. Everything that we read about longevity and an alert mind, recommends daily "exercise." Are you stimulating your mind and letting the light in? This could mean challenging yourself to read more, to engage in intellectual sparring, to tackle a brainteaser or crossword puzzle, to take a course...the possibilities are endless. You just need to make and take the time to build your mind. A keen intellect helps bring lightness. A passion for discovering new things helps you discard heaviness so that you let the light in and let your creativity shine.

Reflect on the state of your intellectual self; decide whether each question gets a 👍 or a 👎.

✹ Do you consciously make time to build your mind?

✹ Are you in touch with the things that stimulate your mind and let the light in?

✹ Do you have an understanding of what intellectual or personal growth is for you?

✹ Do you engage in stimulating discourse with others?

So where are you now? Take some time to reflect on how well your intellectual self is serving your lightness. What did you discover? You may want to take a moment to jot down some notes.

"Intellectual growth should commence at birth and cease only at death"
—Albert Einstein

Darkness: Steer clear

You must know people who always see the negative side of things. Negativity can be beliefs, stories, or the result of a series of bad experiences. It can also just be the way we're wired from birth. Lightness is about knowing that we have a negative side, but also knowing that we can pull ourselves back from it and say, "Wait a minute! I want the light. I want to be positive, and I want to see what the possibilities are. I will look at what's rational and real."

It's important to consider what "dark" looks and feels like for you. I'm going to recall that trucker: It's sad, it's scary, and for some people it is hopelessness. How many times have you heard someone say, "I failed before, so I might as well not even try." That's hopelessness. Dark is de-energizing and dispirited. "It's no use." Here we're talking about the darkest of the dark, but there are nuances to darkness.

At its very worst, darkness is desperation. When we go from being positive and optimistic to a dark place, it saps our energy, it saps our self-esteem, and it saps our power. Our encounters with darkness can be irrational. In a minor way, I know about irrational fear and how it can render us helpless. I have an irrational fear of mice. (Don't laugh!) I mean, I think about how much bigger I am than a mouse, and I know it's irrational. But if I saw one right now, it would instantly take all my power away. I'd be frozen in place! Fear that is irrational often goes back to your childhood. I know mine does.

A delicate balance…

When the scales are tipped toward the negative and you lose your sense of balance, do a reality check. Ask, "What's the worst that could happen? What's the best that could happen?" If you're weighed down with negativity it really brings you to the dark. You might feel overwhelmed, passive and numb, or burned out. When your balance is tipped toward to the dark, it doesn't keep you safe. Actually, it keeps you on unsafe ground, because you are afraid to try new things that might be wonderful for you. I'm not talking about physical or monetary safety. I mean that you're not getting into the possibilities that you could have.

> "I always try to balance the light with the heavy; a few tears of human spirit in with the sequins and the fringes."
> —Bette Midler

Some of us are full of unbridled optimism, and we have to balance that. Call me guilty! The more I work with clients on Lightness of Being, the more I work on myself. I realize that achieving a balance and tilting toward the light will give you the right perspective on your life. But periods of darkness help balance that bright optimism; they serve a purpose. They will actually help you tilt toward optimism and away from negativity. The balance between the two is what keeps you whole and safe.

Sometimes the greatest Light comes after darkness. Sometimes we must get dark before we can see the light. We must be able to envision and understand the dark. We must understand what negativity does to us, what it looks and feels like, before we can truly recognize and embrace the light. After all, without a dark night sky, we wouldn't be able to see the stars!

Darkness is associated with:	Lightness is associated with:
Loss of confidence	Self-honor
Avoiding success	Acceptance
Low self-esteem	Tolerance
Negativity	Courage
Fear	Confidence
Closed-mindedness	Optimism
Dispiritedness	Creativity
Timidity	Hope
Being stuck	Flexibility
Rigidity	Openness
Stress	Calm

You have heard these before…

Give these time-tested expressions some thought. What is their personal meaning for you? Let your imagination and your inner light help you in considering them.

"You are the light of my life!"

"Light my fire."

"I've seen the light."

"He's light on his feet."

"This little light of mine, I'm gonna let it shine."

> Just for this week:
>
> Pick one that is particularly meaningful for you. Set aside a special time of day and reflect on it. See what surfaces for you! See what steps you want to take!

A cautionary tale about Sally

This story is about making decisions with an awareness of how light influences facts, choices, and intuition.

Sally is successful, brilliant, and talented. She is known and sought after in her field. Sally lives in San Francisco and works in a high-pressure job that holds promise but also overwhelming challenges. She's in a 24/7 environment. "All I do is work, eat, and sleep!"

But take a look back and get to know Sally before she moved to the West Coast. About seven months ago, she was working for a well-known company in the Southeast. She had an excellent job and was highly compensated. The company had been doing well but was slipping a little. Many of her colleagues were leaving and going to a sexy new startup. She stayed where she was because she had meaningful work and felt that at her age (40ish), it might be safer to stay put.

Sally was quite satisfied with all aspects of her life. She was very much in touch with what gave her light and she made conscious choices to maintain her lightness. The startup company was making overtures to her but she kept saying, "No. I have everything I want where I am. I'm really happy. I have balance in my life." The company she was with was having a bit of trouble but was still secure. Working there honored her values and her need for light.

Watch the Light begin to dim for Sally.

Sally was eventually seduced by the praise of the startup managers. They would "love to have her... she was so great." They promised her a reduced work week, rather than the 60+ hours everyone else was working. "You'd love the challenge." Money was not an issue. After months of saying no, Sally suddenly decided to take the job. Why on earth did she do such an abrupt about-face?

> **We all have our personal dragons and those things that can move us to a place of darkness. We have to recognize them and deal with them.**

What's weighed Sally down for her entire professional career is the nagging thought that maybe she's not that smart, maybe she's not as good as her colleagues with Ivy League educations and who didn't have to work their way through college. But the new company spoke to her inner child, telling her how good she was, and it was that message that overrode the voice saying, "Maybe you're not good enough. Maybe you're not really that smart." She took the new position.

Seven months ago, there was balance in Sally's life; seven months later, she sold her house and relocated to San Francisco. Now she's in the office, not working from home.

She starts at 5am and gets back whenever. The cost of living in San Francisco is greater than in the Southeast. She now has a mortgage. The new company has tight deadlines. She only has two weeks vacation for the next couple of years. She's no longer playing golf. She left the church she was active in and has not had time to join a new one. She is eating badly and has gained back almost all the weight she'd recently lost. She's under incredible stress. Her spouse remained back east and they see one another infrequently. Family is not there as it was for Sally.

Sally does love the challenge but she has lost the balance she once had. And when you loose balance, the stress can become complicated.

The point to take away from Sally's story is that you have to know and discover what gives you light, and you have to acknowledge and honor it. You also have to be keenly aware of what causes darkness. What or who are the devils, the dragons, which cause you to give up your lightness and put you in a place of unbalance? Sally knew what gave her light, but she allowed herself to be derailed by those gremlins. The weakness and weight for her was a sense of inferiority that she held onto.

We're not saying Sally is a failure. She's not. She working it out; she'll stay with the job, but it has taken a great toll on her. It will take her a while to get the lightness back. Let's hope this will be one of those wonderful learning experiences where Sally will actually reconnect with what gives her light by realizing what causes her darkness.

Hopefully, she'll see how that dragon she's carried for so long undermines her values. Hopefully, she'll say, "Stop in the name of love: love for myself. I am not honoring my whole package. I am not feeding my Lightness of Being, and I do not have a good level of fulfillment or balance in my life." She's smart: She'll find her equilibrium and let the light in. And that light will give her clarity of vision.

What we're hoping for Sally is that one day she'll say, "OK.

Enough. This is it!" And on that day she will say to this new company, "I love the challenge of working here, but I'm no longer available 24/7. I need to have a life. How can we work this out?" Once she does that, she'll know she has truly lifted that weight of feeling inferior, of feeling she is not as good as her colleagues. She'll slay a dragon!

See Sally. See Sally go—down

Look at the subtle descending spiral that sent Sally to a place of discouragement and loss of confidence.

Has a high degree of contentment in all areas of her life, from job to leisure.

Bosses express sincere appreciation of her skills and talents at work.

Decision to stay put after colleagues leave company.

Relocation and new job holds potential.

Work is demanding but challenging.

Thinks she may not keep up.

Feels other are smarter.

Sleeps too little.

Eats too much.

Not smart.

See Sally. See Sally go—up

Now let's look at the pattern of thinking that could enable Sally to reframe her thinking, reverse the descending spiral, and return to a place where she feeling competent and confident.

It is my responsibility to balance work and play so that I maintain myself as a well-rounded person.

I am empowered and in control of the decisions about my career, my health, and my life.

The risks I've taken and the sacrifices I've made are good and will reward me in time.

I have an obligation to communicate openly and frequently about my needs.

I can negotiate the demands my job places on me.

I've earned the trust of peers through quality work.

Others are smart, and I can learn from them.

My experience is valued.

I'm smart enough.

I'm me.

What is lightness for you?

In the next few pages, you'll have a chance to make notes on what makes you feel light. Let me first share with you my own feelings and the feeling expressed by others.

> I am light when my to do list is blank and I am organized.

> I'm light when I spend time with my grandchild.

> I feel light when I'm completely caught up and there are no demands on my time.

> I'm light when I'm working on a creative project. I can be painting, writing, cutting or gluing for a collage — I'm totally focused and lost in time and space. My soul doesn't even touch the ground!

> There is a moment when I feel light, and it's a physical thing. It starts in my stomach. Warmth travels or floods through my whole body. It is a feeling of elation, joy, really. I get that feeling sometimes just looking at my kids with awe and gratitude. I think, "How beautiful they are! And I made them!"

> Lightness is being able to pull it all together. When I'm faced with a challenge — I mean way over my head — I stretch, I work hard: I use skills I didn't even know I had. I succeed through my own will and determination. What a good feeling! I feel like I could take on anything. I'm confident and energized.

Imp test on lightness that animates.

Give yourself 16.6 points for each affirmative answer. Need a calculator?

1. You know what your dark side looks like.

2. You are keenly aware of what snuffs out your light.

3. You know with certainty what let's light in for you.

4. You can articulate the names of people, conditions, or situations that undermine your sense of well-being or competence.

5. You embrace the tools that help you get in touch with actions and behaviors that enable a Lightness of Being.

6. You have discovered your own unique light.

If you scored at least 16.6, give yourself a treat. Then get busy, because you have so much more to discover.

Imp Wisdom!

Celebrate whenever there is even the teeniest reason!

Lightness for You…

Sit comfortably with your eyes closed. Relax and breathe easily. Imagine yourself totally embraced by lightness.

1. How does lightness make you feel? Bring to mind a picture that you associate with how you feel.

2. Describe how you look when you're feeling light.

3. What changes happen in your body that you are aware of? Do you sound different?

4. Are there others in this light space? How are they?

5. Can you compare this feeling with similar feelings or states of being that you've experienced?

6. What could occur that would amplify your feeling of lightness?

Do a "Light Check"

1. Where are you tilted on the light/dark meter? What is causing the tilt?

2. Are you being weighed down or are you feeling free? Explain.

3. What's light-taking or light-giving for you right now?

4. What will you do to achieve your desired balance between lightness and darkness?

Listen to your heart

1. What do you hear when you listen to the voice inside you?

2. What does it mean?

3. What sustains your soul, lifts your spirits, and takes hold of your heart?

4. What do you want to change NOW about your physical, spiritual, and/or intellectual self?

5. What do you want to move away from?

6. What do you want to do to move toward?

Take action!

Amp it up! 5 things you can do to increase the light:

1. Call a light-giving friend.

2. Pick one of your light-giving activities and just do it. Don't think about whether you have the time!

3. Put Post-its with "light-givers" on them around your house, office or wherever you spend a lot of time.

4. Say this affirmation: "I am filled with light and feel so energized and free."

5. Make up your own personal mantra to say when you want to summon up the feeling of lightness.

CHAPTER 6

Dragons

In the previous chapter, you read about Sally and how she was seduced by her own gremlins or, as I like to call them… dragons. Those seductive little creatures can have great control and influence over your life…if you let them. Vanquishing the little buggers gets easier and easier the more we understand and choose what gives us light and limit what takes it away. Dragons are definitely light-zappers who can take over and prevent you from living your best life

Dragons will aid and abet your "stuckness" as they help you to rationalize why you are not leaving the awful job, why you should not retire, why you have to keep seeing dreadful Aunt Mabel, even though she makes you feel bad about yourself every time. You get the picture.

Face your dragons

Your personal dragons are the obstacles or barriers that keep you from moving forward. Consider these dragons very broadly, from tangible situations to individuals, from beliefs to inner voices.

You have created a vision for your life, and to get and stay on the path of your vision, you need to know and recognize your dragons when they start firing up. Some have been with you for ages and are devious…often in the guise of a wise advisor. Some derive from situations that you're in. Consider this: Some may be opportunities in disguise.

Once you know them, put them in their place and refuse to give them power. They are to be removed, overcome, or circumvented if you are to proceed on the path you've chosen. Think of them as dragons that need to be slain. No one says this is easy.

You need pluck and courage to get them out of your life!

Some dragons heard from coaching clients...

" From as far back as I can remember, my father was always telling me to be satisfied with a steady paycheck and not to take chances with the unknown. It has now become my inner voice, and it gets very loud and insistent when I think about quitting my job and going back to school."
Pete L., MA

"I know that I would be so much happier living in a warmer climate, living close to the beach. The sea has always been a place where I can unleash my creative juices. But my parents are getting older, and I need to stay close to them, don't I? Isn't that what a good daughter would do? It feels selfish to want to move away."
Jane J., NH

"There is no way I could afford to pursue my dream of opening my own catering business. I have too many obligations and no spare cash. That's it...I am not even going to think about it anymore. Enough!!"
Pat B., CT

"Don't bite off more than you can chew! I really believe this. Where is my head at in thinking that I can be a foster parent to this lovable little child? The past has taught me that I can only handle so much!"
Zoe G., CO

"All of my friends are retiring at that certain age, but I don't want to. I get so much pleasure and fulfillment from my work. There is nothing I can think of that I would rather do with my days. I am starting to feel that there is something wrong with me and that I should apologize for continuing to work when I could comfortably (financially) retire. I thoroughly enjoy my vacations and my free time. If one more person asks when are you going to retire? I think I'll scream."

Bonnie R., CT

"What's the use in trying? I never follow through with things. It's a waste of time, money, and energy. Let me just learn to live with the status quo. It's not so bad after all. Dreams are for the young."

Don T, MA

"Exercising and taking long walks on the beach have always helped me to keep my life in balance and to keep my negativity (a family trait) in check. It also helps me to be more creative, not to mention healthy and strong. I guess you might say exercise is one of my light-givers. Two months ago I had a fall and did extensive damage to my right foot and ankle. Since then I have not been able to exercise, and it is really getting me down."

Donna G., NS Canada

As you can tell, dragons come in all sizes, shapes, and types. To help you think about your own dragons, I have categorized them. Not surprisingly, a dragon can cross or impact all four categories, so don't worry about the label, just about slaying them. A word about slaying...no blood needs to be spilled! When you slay your dragons, you prevent them from holding you back and shutting out your light.

The physical dragons are the easiest to see. People may be challenged by the limitations of their bodies, their weight, their age, or even a perception of how "attractive" or "ugly" they are. Being "too tall or too short "may be thought of as a limit to general attractiveness to the opposite sex. Spend time with a physically challenged person who gets around in a wheelchair or with the aid of leg braces and you may be surprised that he or she does not refer to such limitations as an obstacle.

The behavioral dragons are the things you do that keep you from being where you want to be or from doing what you feel and know you should be doing. Your good intentions are often undermined by the person you should accept the most— yourself. For one person a dragon might be indecisiveness; for another, passivity. We may feel safer and more accepted by being transparent or invisible. You may be competitive to the point of being combative, always poised to bring your rivals down. Consider some sample behavioral dragons: the grudge-holder, the procrastinator, the gossip, or the clutterer. Lightness asks you to examine your individual stresses, be willing to look at your behaviors, and have the courage to change.

The mind dragons are those deeply held, limiting beliefs about how you should be and how you should act. Some are created from your experiences and some from your belief system. They are the inner voices whispering in your ear: "You can't do this!" or "Better safe than sorry!" or, one of my all-time favorites, "Better a devil you know than one you don't."

These charmers and seducers often sound so knowing and caring that you may naturally fall for them. Their strength comes from the measure of truth that they contain. Think about the comment: "You shouldn't take on any more commitments, you have too much to do already" or your parent's caution not to speak to strangers. Slaying a mind dragon may be as simple as taking the time to discover what makes you happy and what your strengths are, and a firm determination to enjoy life. Overcome mind dragons with determination. Take a good, long look at the way your mind works and give it a workout!

Let me add here that a few of you may be in such a defeated or negative space that you need the help of a professional. When it comes to overwhelming grief or depression, you owe it to yourself to see a therapist. Give yourself that gift.

The wallet dragons are the financial limitations you have or the financial choices you make that keep you from pursuing the life you want to live. Nothing grinds us down quicker than our concern over finances. Talk about worry! Whether it's medical bills, tuition, mortgage payments, loss of a second income, credit card debt, or the demands of just making ends meet, the lack of a stable financial picture is the cause of many a sleepless night. This dragon needs long-term planning, creative options, or perhaps a mind-shift to overcome. So much of our financial health depends on our job, our spending habits, and the general state of the economy. Our ability to earn and save is affected by education, opportunity, and goals, but most of all by discipline.

"Fairy tales are more than true; not because they tell us that dragons exist, but because they tell us that dragons can be beaten"
~ G. K. Chesterton

Jenny's story

One day, six months ago, Jenny came into work and learned that her job had been eliminated and she was getting just two weeks of severance pay. She was devastated, because she really enjoyed her position and the restaurant where she worked was training her to be their sommelier. Jenny was passionate about wine and learned all she could about it in her spare time. She loved nothing better than to suggest a bottle of wine to customers and have them be thrilled with the selection. Their smiles and delight really buoyed her up.

Jenny's first order of business (once she got over the initial shock) was to step back and think about what she really wanted to do with her life. Although she loved the restaurant business, the long, late hours were a detriment to her personal life. When she considered the whole experience, what she discovered was that her love for the business was really "all about the wine." What she also discovered through many long conversations with her very enlightened spouse, Hank, was that she had always wanted to be a teacher. At first blush (not blush wine) it didn't seem as if these were compatible loves.

But wait...can you see the dragon slaying taking place?

Jenny contacted the local school board and discovered they needed substitute teachers in biology. It would require some legwork and some paperwork, but within a few weeks she was on the official sub list and was getting called almost every day.

But what about her passion for wine? Jenny paired her love of wine with a love of teaching and parlayed it into her own

108

business venture. On any given weekend afternoon and some evenings, you will find her in front of a roomful of people, helping them learn about wine. The seminars are such a success that she now has waiting lists. Word of Jenny's talks has become so widespread that she is now being asked by corporations to tutor rising young executives on the do's and don'ts of fine dining and ordering wine.

Often, Hank accompanies Jenny, and they have found that they work very well together. The couple doesn't know what the next step is, but they are more than ready to answer when opportunity knocks on their door.

"Heros take journeys, confront
dragons, and discover the treasure
of their true selves"
~ Carol Lynn Pearson

Slay your dragons

Loving the whole package that is you is absolutely central to slaying your dragons. Slaying them means that you will not let them stop you from your chosen path, that you will use them to understand risks, that you will overcome them to live your life as you choose, that you will not give them power, and that you will find the opportunities lurking behind the smoke from their fire.

Just recognizing that they exist and are our biggest barriers to moving toward the light is the first step in putting them in their place, to figuring out how to deal with them. A word to the wise: The dragons are around for a reason, and often that is to help us be mindful of risk. Sometimes I consider them flashing yellow lights that say "Take a moment and think before you leap." Just don't let them keep you stuck in place.

Obstacles are ever-present and often daunting. The fact that we continue to thrive in spite of them is a testament to our strength as human beings and heroic individuals.

Dragon Slaying 101:

Love and embrace your passions and values.

Know who and what your dragons are.

Recognize how much fire power they have, and how much is just smoke.

Deal with them by saying "So what?"

Put yourself ahead of them.

See what opportunities they are hiding from you.

Respect them and move on!

Be a hero. Slay your dragons!

Imp Wisdom!

Your dragons may just be smoke!

Challenge assumptions that put your dreams on hold.

You have the power and the might to slay your dragons!

Identify your dragons and get the lowdown on them.

Think about the changes you want to make in your life. What gets in the way when you consider making those changes?

Complete the following sentences:

> Every time I start to think about making a change, I get stopped by:

> This stops me because:

Dragon, be gone!

Now that you've defined them, let's work on slaying the fiercest dragons.

1. For your _____ Dragon, what steps can you take to put out the fire?

   And what will it do for you?

2. Select another dragon and put into words why it has no power over you.

   Now that you know it has no power, what actions will you take to further your vision for your life?

Take Action!

3 things you can do right away to de-power your dragons and move forward on your light path:

1. Ignore a mind or inner-voice dragon and replace it with a positive affirmation. Make up one that works for you and plaster it everywhere!

2. Brainstorm some clever ways to get around a wallet dragon. Be outrageous in your ideas and discover possibilities. Act on one of them.

3. Tell someone about a dragon that is especially thwarting you right now. Ask your friend to help you talk through ways to slay it.

CHAPTER 7

The 2nd L: LIMIT

How often have you said, "I really want to pursue (fill in the blank) but I don't have the time or energy. I'm exhausted from (another blank)?" For many of us, this is a way of life. The idea for Lightness of Being was born out of my own personal frustration over filling my life with too many should-dos rather than want-to-dos. I didn't think I had a choice in the matter! Then the light went on for me. You do have a choice. Conscious choice is the basis for the 2nd L.

You can choose

Limit is not about underachieving. Neither is it about under-committing. Limit, as a tenet of Lightness of Being, is about making self-wise decisions that that will move you along the path of the life you want. You will make the right choices for yourself to preserve your light, not to shirk your duty or to be selfish. You can make room for the light-givers by limiting, eliminating, or containing the things that weigh you down and dim your light. At many times during your life, weighty situations will be thrust upon you—such as the illness of a loved one, job loss, a too demanding boss—or may occur and grow over time—boredom, marital conflict, too many unnecessary commitments.

When we recognize what limits us, then we can limit it. Think of the things that weigh you down and burden you. It is also about altering the choices you may have made in the past, when your light was dim. I use the word "things" to encompass people, beliefs, tasks, situations…in other words, anything that weighs you down and takes your light.

"Some choices we live not only once but a thousand times over, remembering them for the rest of our lives"
~ Richard Bach

Limit is a powerful ally in the quest for what you want for your life. Limit is based on the fundamental principle that you do have options, and you have the right to choose which options to take…all in service to the whole package that is you. It's about focus and definition.

It takes courage to act on your choices!

When we think of Lightness of Being and getting rid of the things that weigh us down and keep us from doing what we truly want to do and are meant to do, we get a sense of what is keeping us from being our true selves. This means taking on the things you want. It's consciously choosing. How often have you heard yourself say, "Life got in the way?" Yes…life does get in the way, and as a result you must focus on the things you really want to be with.

Recognize the burdens that are self-inflicted or are not contained and how they prevent you from living your best life each and every day.

Limit, eliminate, or contain what you cannot be with!

Make the Light choices for yourself:

The work you do

The people you are with

The activities you pursue

How you spend your money

How you spend your time

What you say NO to

What you say YES to.

Introducing the Limit Imp!!

Allow another side of your imp to encourage you to fully embrace the 2nd L:

Limit

**Limit the light-takers;
Make room for the light-givers, the energizers**

Consciously choose what you want in your life

Eliminate what you don't want

Do what you are comfortable managing

Plan ways to alter your thinking

Take steps to make time for what you want

Try on new habits

Heavy tales…

As you read through these stories, think about what choices each person could make to let in more light. What is keeping them from what they want, what could they limit, and how might they go about it?

"I honestly can't remember the last time I spent an evening with my closest friends. Between the demands of my job and trying to be a good mother to my three kids, I don't have a moment to spare for frivolous activities."
Joan R., MA

"Just heard about a great job in my field, and I do believe that I am more than qualified for it. It would get me out of this dead-end job, and the starting salary could mean a big difference to my life style. The cutoff for applications is Wednesday. My resume is outdated and needs some work before I could submit it. I doubt if I'll have the chance to get it revised before Wednesday. Besides, they are probably flooded with great candidates."
Sammy L., NC

"When my mother became bedridden last year, my life got put on hold. My whole focus has been on her, and though I love her dearly, I am worn out and not feeling too perky myself. My siblings and my children all offer to help out, but Mother prefers my care because I am the closest to her and I really know what she likes. I hope that I still remember how to play the piano...it has been too long."
Pam S., OR

"If you had told me 10 years ago that I would come to think of Jane as a toxic friend, I would have wondered what you were talking about. Every encounter with her (and there are a lot of them) leaves me feeling just plain bad. She has a way of sounding well-meaning, but somehow it turns into criticism of my life, my job, my vacation choice, my spouse...you name it. I want this to stop, but I don't know what to do. We have been friends for over 10 years. That's a long time!"
Diane C., CT

As you think through what you want to limit, consider that one of the reasons we often cannot even approach limiting is because of our belief system or because of how we want to be perceived. Sometimes your dragons are breathing heavy fire your way. Sometimes you have lost sight of what you value and love!

Not one more lunch with…

So here's the thing… Aunt Mabel is your aunt and you value family. But face it she is a shrew and usually puts you down while you silently fume and also pay for lunch. For about two days before the monthly luncheon, you feel overwhelmed, weighed down, and dispirited. This sounds pretty dramatic, but I'm willing to wager that each and every one of you has an Aunt Mabel in your life. And it's pretty clear what this does to you.

How did this happen?

Curiously enough, many of us spend planned time with these light-zappers with no idea of how these dates came to be. They just keep recurring. So what can you do about it?

Let's acknowledge that a situation such as the Aunt Mabel one has many nuances and facets, and there may be other people who will be impacted or who won't like it, if you change the pattern. So what?? This is your life: You are not being unkind or immoral or evil or selfish. In honor of the whole package, you must put some limits on this relationship.

> ## The 5 C's of Limit:
>
> Clarify the light-taker and his/her/its impact.
>
> Choose what you want/don't want.
>
> Commit to the limit plan; be aware of the risks and benefits
>
> Carry out your decision.
>
> Celebrate your courage

Let's see how one might limit the Aunt Mabel relationship.

1. Clarify: You are always exhausted and a bit intimidated for several days prior to the luncheon.

2. Choose: You do want to spend some time with Aunt Mabel, but not every month. Twice a year feels right. It would allow you to plan something special and memorable for both of you.

3. Commit: Make a plan, prepare for the discussion, and tell a friend. Mabel might get angry and say that you have changed, but she won't cut you out of her life. You may actually look forward to seeing her. Consider other people who will weigh in on this and try to get you to be your old self. Think about how you will handle them.

4. Carry out: Let Aunt Mabel know that you want to spend quality time with her, perhaps a show and lunch.. Be firm yet loving and make specific plans for your next outing together. Remove the monthly lunches from your calendar.

5. Celebrate: Tell your friend about the decision. Eat a bonbon!

Three cheers for courage!!!!

A CIO's tale

Claire is the CIO of a midsize corporation. She is an exceptionally qualified professional as well as an experienced, caring manager. She is looked to as a leader, someone who can be trusted. She has extremely high ethical and work standards. She is compassionate and has a great sense of humor. She is adept at forming and sustaining relationships with a variety of people. Claire could find some way to connect with anyone from Pablo Picasso to a counter worker at McDonald's. She is also a very talented artist—who has not picked up a paintbrush in 10 years!

Claire is weighed down by an ever-growing to-do list and a crowded work calendar. She is methodical and works best when she can devote herself to a piece of work and concentrate on it uninterrupted.

She is operating under the belief that to be a "good" leader and manager, she has to meet with each person on her staff once a week (the manager who mentored her instilled this belief). She started this practice two years ago and is still at it.

Burdened by her belief that once a week was the right thing to do, she never sought to do anything about it… she just kept coming into work earlier and staying later. Claire is torn between her desire to be there for her employees and her need for time to get her own work done.

Your thoughts?

* What does Claire have to rethink, given what we've said about lightness?

* What specifically weighs Claire down?

* What really weighs her down that she hasn't come to grips with?

* What benefits can Claire expect if she commits to focus on being light?

* What risks might she have to take?

* What immediate changes would you suggest she make?

* What might be some of the consequences of her actions?

"Life is a sum of all your choices."
~Albert Camus

It is not always so simple...

Limiting our beliefs and habits or ingrained practices often requires slaying a dragon or two. This is especially true for the dragons that are based on "old" beliefs or rules. Many of the rules were made by your parents, to protect you.

Think of how such rules have held people back in life and deprived them of some really wonderful relationships. As adults, many have translated the warning not to talk to strangers (a favorite among parents) to mean: Don't trust strangers.

Limit involves so many facets. You limit in honor of the love you have for yourself, in honor of your passions and your values, in honor of your own lightness. Think about the things you cannot be with and what you are willing to do about them.

Always remember to ask:
"What's the worst that can happen?"

The worst is probably insignificant in light of the best that can happen!

IMP Wisdom!

You know exactly how you want to spend your time.

You know what you want and need to limit to make your vision a reality.

You have the power, the right, and the stuff to make decisions on behalf of living your best life!

The top 5!!

Make a list of the top 5 things you want to:
    a) Limit or completely eliminate from your life and
    b) What limiting them will do for you.

1.   a)
      b)

2.   a)
      b)

3.   a)
      b)

4.   a)
      b)

5.   a)
      b)

Time to look back before going forward

Take a look through some of the things you have learned about yourself and select one area that you want to rearrange, change, or limit.

1. What are your priorities? How do they match up to the pieces of your life?

2. How have they shifted over the past year?

3. What circumstances shape your priorities?

4. How readily can you change them?

5. Do you frequently change your priorities to suit what you enjoy doing?

Take action!

4 things you can choose to do to let in the light.

1. Look at your calendar for the month. Pick something that you will limit or eliminate. Don't forget the 5 C's!

2. Pick one behavior you want to change. Don't analyze it, just make the change and then revel in what this does for you.

3. Do something by tomorrow to ratchet up your satisfaction level with one piece of your life.

4. Get in touch with your limit imp and see how many light-zappers you can eliminate or contain within the next week. Once you've done it, remember to celebrate!!

CHAPTER 8

The 3rd L: LAUGH

Great news...laughing makes you stronger, friendlier, and sexier. This news is based on loads of anecdotal data and scientific research also. Studies have shown that humor and laughter may influence health and can even be of help in dealing with pain. We all know that laughter and cheerfulness can help you deal with life's ups and downs. Nothing shows self-confidence like the ability to laugh at yourself.

An amusing image…

At its very core, laugh is about appreciating life and feeling the energy that resonates from positivity. Think about something that makes you smile and lights you up from inside. The ability to summon up positive, happy, playful images can make all the difference in your mood. So many happy images are based on animals or young children. Could it be because they don't have any cares beyond the present moment?

"Whenever I want to get out of a funk, one of the images that I summon is of my 4 year-old niece's ballet recital. I can still see 15 little ballerinas in their tutus going in about five different directions. Their innocence is infectious, and I smile just thinking about that evening and those adorable little girls."
Ann G., CT

"My favorite goes back about 10 years and it is still with me… perhaps because I've used it so often. It is the image of a litter of golden retrievers running around, tumbling together and feeling safe because Mama was nearby. They tug at one another, wrestle, and fall instantly asleep whenever they want. They are pure pleasure, warmth, and playfulness".
John Z., CA

"Life must be lived as play."
~ Plato

Introducing the Laugh Imp

Allow another side of your imp to encourage you to fully embrace the 3rd L:

Laugh
Laugh and play more often.
Live in appreciation of life.

Take delight in simple things.

Make some mischief.

Laugh out loud.

Escape from routine.

Make pleasure, joy, and gratitude your trio.

Break some rules.

Get in touch with your inner IMP!

Be playful, creative and impish

An effective weapon…

"The human race has only one really effective weapon, and that is laughter."
~ Mark Twain

When I first read this quote, it reminded me of all the people I've met who deal so well with life's peaks and valleys. Their humor, cheerfulness, and laughter are perfect weapons. You have to really love a weapon that does no damage, but rather does so much good. Laughter can help you through some of the darkest and most stressful times in your life. So arm yourself with the weapon of laughter and humor.

Laughter will let light in. It allows you to let go. Think about it: How can you laugh so hard that you have tears in your eyes and still be thinking about anything? You will only be experiencing.

Humor yourself…

Some people are born with a highly developed sense of humor; others have to work at it. I urge you to find some humor in your life each and every day.

"Humor is just another defense against the universe."
~ Mel Brooks

We all know that you can't laugh away a very serious situation, but humor can help you to cope with it better. It will let in some light and might also help you to see the situation in another light.

Lighten up!

Truly get in touch with the Laugh side of your Imp. This playful, mischievous person inside you will help you to adjust your reactions to things. See yourself as the Imp and react accordingly.

You may only be smiling on the inside, but who cares! You have a great grin going, and you feel the humor bubbling up inside. Make your Imp a part of your daily journey.

Get in touch with your Imp and have a ball!

Lighten Up!

Limit what zaps your light and embrace what gives you light.

There is nothing like a laugh to bring some light into your life.

You can adjust your thinking to see the humorous side of most situations.

Don't take yourself too seriously.

Create humorous situations...don't wait for humor to pop into your life!

IMP Wisdom!

Laughter is the best medicine.

Research supports the need for laughter and playfulness.

You know you want to do this.

Go forth and whoop it up.

You have the power, the right, and the stuff to enjoy life!

What makes you laugh, smile, and feel lighthearted?

Name some of these things and how great they make you feel.

1.

2.

3.

4.

5.

Keep going…

The trio of pleasure, joy, and gratitude

Consider the trio in your life. What are or have been your joys and pleasures, and for what do you have gratitude? Give this exercise the time it deserves and be aware that the light will be turned on for you as they surface.

Take action!

You are such an Imp.
6 things you can do right away to get the laughter
going and put some lightness in your life:

1. Watch an episode a day of some great oldies,
   such as "I Love Lucy" or "The Three Stooges."
   Let yourself go and have some belly laughs

2. Make up some knock-knock jokes and tell
   them to at least one person a day for two weeks.
   You may not be able to stop yourself!

3. Create a memory bank of "smile images." Look
   around you and commit some playful situations to
   memory. They will help you lighten up on dark
   days!

4. Wear a mismatched pair of earrings or socks (loud
   and colorful). You will get a laugh out of people
   pretending not to notice. Remember, you are an
   Imp and you are not worried about what they
   will think!

5. Tell a friend or two that you are going to spend the
   day in play, and later tell them about it. Invite them
   along if you want!

6. Set up a trio board (pleasure, joy and gratitude);
   check it out each day, and add to it often.

Live it!

CHAPTER 9

Your Light Path

Set your own direction

You need a compass, a map, or a plan. Only you know where you are headed and what your personal vision is. You've assessed what weighs you down and what lifts you up and keeps you light. You are aware of what you need to change. You know that it is up to you to ensure that you keep moving in the direction that makes you feel more satisfied, more creative, and more delighted with life.

You decide for yourself all things relating to your life. No one is an island; you can't ignore others who may depend on you or on whom you depend. However, once your values are owned and your direction is chosen, you are entitled by free will to decide and direct your future.

> **Three factors are critical:**
>
> **Empowerment**
>
> **Choice**
>
> **Action**

Getting "permission" may have been appropriate when you were 16 years old and got a driver's permit. Asking a partner for a "sabbatical" from work to raise a child is reasonable, because the time off has significant financial implications and impacts both of you. Making changes in your own best interest will, by courtesy, require discussion and, in some cases, joint decision-making, but they should not hinge on someone else's wishes. You set your direction.

"Destiny is no matter of chance. It is a matter of choice. It is not a thing to be waited for, it is a thing to be achieved."
~ William Jennings Bryant

With choice comes responsibility. Not everyone will be pleased or accepting of choices you make. Some choices may mean loss of a job, loss of a friendship or even rejection by family members. Recently, a client of mine said, with great sadness in her voice, "Now that I have started on my doctorate, my family thinks and acts as if I feel that I'm too good for them. There is nothing I can say or do to make them change their thinking. I will just continue to be myself." Becoming your authentic self is at stake, and nothing and no one should stand in your way!

Positioned to Act

You are the CEO of your own life. You are the chief executive officer, who calls the shots and makes the big decisions. You are in control. CEOs will tell you that those enormous paychecks and bonus packages are well-earned because they shoulder a great deal of responsibility. When you're in charge, you live with the decisions you make.

> ## Choices are not always easy:
>
> They come with responsibility.
>
> They harbor risks as well as rewards.
>
> Always ask: "What's the worst that can happen?"
>
> Then ask: "What's the best that can happen?"
>
> Be consequence-savvy and risk-hardy.

Circumstances often thwart your best efforts. Tell a single mother supporting her family or hauling a load of groceries up three flights of stairs that she's the CEO of her life and you may get a look that would stop traffic. Yet at every fork in the road, you make a decision. You choose alone or with other people or wait until circumstances make decisions for you.

If you have trouble making decisions — any decision — learn techniques that can help you. If you are paralyzed by indecision and cannot exert your will, you will not live lightness.

Big and sometimes even small decisions come with consequences and risks, as well as great rewards. If you are risk-averse, you need to become risk-hardy. When making an important, sometimes life-changing decision, sit yourself down and ask: "What's the worst thing that can happen?"

Here is what I recommend:

Write your answers down...it avoids the old ruminating and re-hashing that will hold you back.

Remember to include the good as well as the bad and the ugly.

Take a look at what you have written, check your honesty level, and see where your answers point you.

Once you know the worst, turn to the best.

143

Take a deep breath and ask yourself, "What's the best that can happen?" What will this do for my life? If all else fails, go to the tie-breaker question and ask: "If I don't do this, what will it mean to me and to my life?"

Move from passion to plan

> *"Getting started was the hardest thing for me. I couldn't take that first step. Once the decision was made to relocate to New Mexico to be near my daughter, everything else was easy. Taking the first step is what made all the difference. Slowly everything fell into place."*
> *Anne A., CA*

Examples of **decisions** someone might make in support of their vision. They might decide to:
* Leave a damaging relationship
* Take a course
* Start their own business
* Dump the junk
* Simplify their life
* Change professions
* Relocate
* Buy a new car
* End a dysfunctional friendship
* Change a specific self-limiting behavior
* Buy season tickets to the opera
* Adopt a baby

What's one of your decisions?

Examples of **steps** someone might take in support of a decision. They might:

- Engage a lawyer
- Reconnect with a kindred spirit
- Revise a résumé
- Engage a reliable child-care provider
- Look at condos that are on the market
- Clear out the clutter
- Join a dating service
- Engage a financial planner
- Build a website
- Do some research
- Hire a life coach
- Meet with a real estate agent

What's the first step in support of one of your decisions?

Your preferences…

Consider your personality type and your preferences as a prelude to mapping your path. Are you a big picture thinker who needs to see the "whole" of something before you can decide on the parts? Do you make decisions from intuition and feelings rather than from facts? Do you need to attend to or anticipate every detail before making a move? Your personality type is an important component of how you act.

Ready. Set. Go!

Think of a runner in the starting block, knuckles on the track, and head down, waiting for the "bang" that starts the race. Think of a tennis player in the "ready" position, racket balanced, poised to receive the serve. Getting ready to act on changes means you must position yourself to act.

> **Position yourself to act:**
>
> **Goals and determination are essential.**
>
> **Picture your destination...be clear about your vision for your life.**

The IMP wants to know ...

What are you going to do today?

What are you going to do first thing in the morning?

Light Path to the mountain cabin…

How did Sam (Chapter 2) go about living his vision?
After the "a-ha" vacation, Sam and the family returned to their routine of jobs and school. What was different was that Sam had a vision for his life, and he (with the enthusiastic agreement of his wife) started immediately on his light path.

Being a planner, Sam plotted the major decisions and steps. He called the decisions "luminaries" that would light the path for him. Also being a realist, Sam knew that there would be forks and potholes in the road, choices to make, and risks to take. The first thing he did was get a grip on his financial picture. Some steps he took: had a meeting with his financial planner; had a market study done on his house; learned what his borrowing power was; reviewed family spending habits with his wife. You get the picture!

The next luminary on Sam's path was the type of business he would start. Sam put a lot of effort into studying the options for his business in the mountains: checked what was available for sale; took several trips to evaluate the area and what businesses might be needed; met with three different groups of outdoorsmen to see what they wanted when they went on a fishing trip; visited several thriving fishing locations to see what businesses were successful.

After the business evaluation, Sam decided that the best option was to buy an existing business and re-make it over time into his brilliant concept. He went back to his finances for another hard look. At about that time, he and his wife decided that they would proceed down two paths that would intersect at times and converge at the end. She would walk a path that involved selling their house and relocating the family. His path was all about setting up the business. (Did I mention that Sam is a great delegator?)

I won't bore you with the details, but within a year and a half Sam and the family had relocated to the mountains, owned a successful business, and lived in a warm and homey log cabin.

Light Path to your Vision:

Keep the vision ever present.

Add to the vision as you gain new insights.

Do your homework; don't overdo it.

Take the time to plan; set dates for done-ness.

Realize that forks in the road are often opportunities.

Celebrate your luminaries!

There were some hurdles along the way. Two big ones were the boys' last-minute "dig in our heels" rejection of the whole move, and a severe downturn in the economy, which presented a wide range of risks and unknowns as well as opportunities. But Sam never took his eye off the prize.

"Obstacles are those frightful things you see when you take your eyes off the goal."
~ Henry Ford

Bravo to Sam and his family!!

Your path and plan

As you move forward in applying the ideas of Lightness of Being to your own life, you will want to create some sort of map or light path for yourself. There are several different ways to do this, from the very formal Goals and Action Plan to the unstructured Wish List and To Do's. Use what works best for you.

Regardless of what method you choose, make your changes actionable, with outcomes you can measure. Trace your progress and track your changes.

The IMP recommends:
>To stay the path and focus on actions, use your refrigerator, a bulletin board, or something else that you will look at every day.

Smile at your brilliance!

Recruit a Circle of Support (COS)

We seldom achieve alone. To make a change, whether it is in a job or a relationship, we need support. The greater the challenge, the greater is the need for support. Putting an aging parent in a rest home requires more than personal fortitude; you need the support of a physician, a visiting nurse, a gerontologist, and family members who all must make such an important decision together. Significant weight loss may require a nutritionist, a homeopath, and a cardiologist. Sometimes we just need a friend who knows the challenges we face and cares enough about us to listen or to celebrate our small achievements.

As you set out to make changes or to be transformed in the small (or large!) world you inhabit, enlist help. It will make what you are trying to achieve easier and more long-lasting.

Taking someone into your confidence is not a simple thing. Some steps you may want to take on your own, but others might benefit from the assistance of someone to support your efforts.

Someone who cares about you

COS basics:

Enlist help.

It may be in the form of a professional.

It may be a great friend—or two.

Your COS must care about you and your goal.

Consider their ability to support your agenda.

151

When you enlist help, pick someone who will be committed to your well-being and smart enough not to feel competitive or threatened by your intention to make changes in your life. The buddy's skills must include listening, objectivity, and enthusiasm. Should you want or need a more formal approach to achieving your personal goals, consider engaging a coach to help in sustained and structured ways.

"Don't wait until everything is just right. It will never be perfect. There will always be challenges, obstacles and less than perfect conditions. So what. Get started now. With each step you take, you will grow stronger and stronger, more and more skilled, more and more self-confident and more and more successful."
~ Mark Victor Hansen

Donna's Dream…

Let me tell you about Donna. She was painting a beautiful mural on an alcove in my next-door neighbor's house. She looked down on me—from a 15-foot ladder. She wore gleaming white work clothes, and her wiry gray curls poked out from under a painter's cap. I spent one early spring establishing a perennial garden, and we often chatted when we paused in our work and sipped coffee on my neighbor's veranda.

Donna was a woman on a mission. She worked on every job her boss offered. She often started mixing paints and prepping for the day before 7am and didn't quit until late in the day.

Donna had a plan. She wanted to start her own company, specializing in faux painting and decorative murals, but she also wanted to honor the loyalty the boss gave her when jobs were scarce. Donna knew she needed a better understanding of the business side of things and had enrolled in an evening course, "The Small Business Entrepreneur," at a community college. At the end of each day she did a quick change of clothes and washed up at the local diner before heading off to class. She was hoping to learn not only about how to start and run a new business but how to partner with her boss. With Donna's work ethic, drive, and planning, I expect to see a panel truck one of these days advertising **Donna and Partner Creative Walls**.

Should you adjust your thinking?

Lightness depends on a different way of thinking. This is a new dance: The old steps won't work anymore. The idea of stepping back to take a fresh look at where you want to be is a good one. Sometimes we intend to act but don't. You can waste a whole lifetime "intending" to act when one or two decisions may have made a profound difference.

"Analysis paralysis" sets in when we convince ourselves that we need more time to think, to consider yet another option, to weigh just one more alternative. There is nothing wrong with careful consideration, as long as it is not an excuse for not taking bold action.

> *Carol intended to go back to school and get a degree in accounting. In her present job she feels overlooked by more credentialed people. When she took the job three years ago she felt lucky, full of promise and enthusiasm. Now, Carol feels demoralized. "I am sure that I won't be admitted to college. Besides, the coursework will be too difficult now that I've been away from studies for so long."*

Intention without action does not result in change, Carol!
* Is Carol a victim of her own self-limiting behavior or simply a realist?
* Do you ever find yourself thinking like Carol? What triggers can cause that thinking pattern?

Signs and wonders on the path of lightness

As you begin your personal journey toward change, watch for signs and wonders along the way. We can get rid of the things that are weighing us down, but unless we let light in through the things that make us happy, creative, and fulfilled, we can't move along the lightness path. The helping hand is always there, but you must recognize it and take it.

"Every day you may make progress. Every step may be fruitful. Yet there will stretch out before you an ever-lengthening, ever-ascending, ever-improving path. You know you will never get to the end of the journey. But this, so far from discouraging, only adds to the joy and glory of the climb."
~ Sir Winston Churchill

IMP Wisdom!

When in doubt, take the next small step.

Enjoy the path and all of its twists and turns.

Don't take no for an answer!

Wield the power of your vision!

Luminaries on your light path

1. Write down what needs to happen to move you along your light path.
    Don't worry about the order, just go at it!

2. What should come first, second, third…?
    Don't worry about how you are going to do any of them!

3. Anything else you want to add at the moment?
    Don't worry about adding more; you can do it at any time, and you will!

4. Clean up your list and attach some dates to the first few items.
    Be as bold as you want.
    Use whatever structure works for you.
    My personal favorite is a path with stars marking my steps.

Your personal COS.

Who comes to mind that might be included in a circle of support?

Who could you count on to provide support and encouragement?

Who could offer professional guidance?

Name names!

_____   _____

_____   _____

_____   _____

_____   _____

_____   _____

Now ask them!

Take action!

I am moving. 6 things you can do right away to make progress and light lights on your path:

1. Take your first step, or maybe two or three.

2. Put wonderful reminders on your refrigerator, on your dashboard, on the wall in front of your toilet.

3. Check in with your COS.

4. Celebrate the twists and turns.

5. Break a big step into a couple of small ones and just do them.

6. Read about others who have lived according to their lights and how they did it.

"I am not bound to win, but I am bound to be true. I am not bound to succeed, but I am bound to live up to what light I have."
~ Abraham Lincoln

CHAPTER 10

The 4th L: Live Lightness

You have brilliantly wended your way through this book and embraced your inner Imp…the delightful, loving, and strong sides of your being. Now, let's talk about sustaining lightness in your life—living it every day. The idea is for lightness to become central to your life, to incorporate the 4 Ls into who you are and how you are. You have the wherewithal to generate lightness every day and to focus on feeling, choosing, and being light. It's time to take the understanding you've gained and apply it to everyday living.

Apply the concepts to make the changes or adjustments you intend to make. Pay attention to the subtle changes in the way you think. Any change, whether it's small or life-altering, needs constant attending. Habits have a way of making ruts in our brain that only conscious choice can alter.

Keep reminders handy. Use them daily. Create a mantra that you repeat throughout the day. Something as simple as, "honor yourself" can become a powerful reminder to live lightness.

"opportunities multiply as they are seized."
~ Sun Tze

"It felt so good to get to know my values and to really discover my passion in life. Who would have thought that I love learning different languages? My dream has always been to travel through Europe, effortlessly going from country to country and speaking as if I were a native. I have already mastered French and just started on German. I have this fabulous plan to travel to France, Germany, and Belgium next year and mix it up with the locals. But all of a sudden I am getting sidetracked by other priorities in my life. Lately I have been fretting that I may not be able to live my vision."
Joan R., RI

Introducing the Live Lightness Imp!!

Your imp encourages you to fully embrace the 4th L:

Live Lightness

Live lightness every day.

Stay focused on your light path.

Act on your own behalf.

Keep self-limiting behaviors in check.

Keep learning, discovering, and growing

Picture it, feel it, seek it.

Embrace the energy!

Awareness is your new best friend….

Use the heightened self-awareness you've gained. Use lightness reflections as insight into your life experiences and how they make you unique. Keep a deep appreciation of who you are right now, and of the infinite potential you possess.

"In theory, there is no difference between theory and practice. But in practice, there is."
~ Yogi Berra

Awareness requires searching your dark corners and embracing those spaces that need light. Whether they are the daily challenges of living or the intense and unexpected stresses that flood your life, you need to examine the pools of light as well as areas of darkness. This demands that you read the clues when you are straying from your light path.

Watch for signs that may mean you are on the verge of being overwhelmed. If you know about the waves that can swamp your boat, you can correct your course. It is when you are not fully awake, dozing, distracted and distraught, that you can flounder without knowing why.

Side Trips

Don't let a side trip trip you up!

Take a few moments and check out what's sidetracking you.

Then get back on the path you have chosen.

163

Watch for the dawn....

Earlier in this book you thought about what causes you to feel darkness, that area of no light. You may have said that darkness is a feeling of being lost, so confused that you don't know what to do, where to turn, or how to break thorough frustration or apathy.

Remember: You have an enormous capacity for dealing with the obstacles that present themselves. These can be as mild as a missed appointment or as profound as the loss of a job, a severe illness, or heartbreak. Consider the resilience of the human spirit and how powerful an ally this is. You are stronger than you think!

As you become more aware and accepting that there will be periods of darkness, you can direct your conscious desire to be light and actually shorten those periods. You will learn to balance a temporary period of darkness with your own brilliant incandescence. Remember, without periods of darkness, we could not fully appreciate lightness.

**Distractions and derailments will occur.
So what...life happens!**

Keep focused on the love

Be prepared for consequences and act with courage. You surely have people in your life who like you just the way you are and want to keep you just as you are. They are comfortable with the familiar you. For them, change is threatening. As you begin to rearrange your priorities and to honor the whole wonderful package that is you, you will need courage to stick to what you intend, regardless of the discomfort of someone else. Be aware of dragons and stressors. Find ways to lessen or mitigate them as best you can.

> **Be ready to live lightness every day!**
>
> **Act with courage.**
>
> **Engage your circle of support.**
>
> **Continue to widen your circle.**
>
> **Take small steps as well as large ones.**
>
> **Celebrate your accomplishments!**

Engage your circle of support to help you stay on track. Don't hesitate to add to your circle. Guidance and support are essential to change. Who are our guides? Who are our champions, who cheer us on when our courage flags? Who believes in you when it seems few others do? Have you ever felt "guided"?

Maybe it was a teacher who believed that your ability could be s-t-r-e-t-c-h-e-d; the personal trainers who envisioned a strong, flexible body instead of a sagging, overweight one; the partner whose "You can do it!" was a turning point in your self-confidence. Give yourself a pat on the back frequently. You deserve rewards for living your best life now. Acknowledge your accomplishments with deep appreciation — often. Keep a bottle of bubbly on ice for those moments!

Size does not matter. Forward movement does. Whether large or small, take steps. Begin with small, incremental ones and then move on to greater challenges as you progress. Scrap steps that don't work and substitute ones that do. You will be amazed at the surge of confidence you will enjoy.

Love:

Yourself—body, mind, and spirit.

Your values.

Your wants and needs.

Your priorities.

Your passions.

Your pursuits.

Your limitations.

A light lunch

I asked a group of friends who gather every other month to connect, encourage, catch up, laugh, and enjoy lunch to talk about lightness. They have been following the progress of *The Lightness of Being You*, and I engaged them in a simple exercise. We went around the table and each person completed this sentence:

"If I were living light, I'd be more…"

Tara went first: "If I were living light I'd be more dedicated to my thesis. I'd have finished with my Ph.D. and I'd be in a teaching position at some local college. The boys would have a great day-care arrangement, and I could take up running again."

Joan said, "If I were living light I'd be more confident about making a decision about where to live. I'd have smart people around who could advise me on the best options for my income and my family responsibilities. I'd feel ready and prepared to relocate if necessary without worrying about making a bad choice, or about getting any flak from my relatives."

Leslie said, "I'd be freer to ask for what I want and reject what I don't want at work. I'd ask for a whole bundle of new projects, and I'd be at every single one. I'd be successful. I'd be the best, most creative person in the whole place!"

Bruce finished the sentence this way: "I'd be more settled. I'd have my kids back. I'd live in Florida near my dad, and I'd be doing work that I love."

Judy said, "I would retire and pursue the hobby I have been putting off for years. I have always wanted the time and flexibility to put together my genealogy, to walk in the path of my ancestors and to get in touch with my roots."

I believe, and I told the group so, that each of them had the capacity to be lighter, beginning right after lunch. (How's that for an oxymoron?)

Lightness is associated with behaviors that foster growth. Make a note of the people who help you feel light. Choose people who energize you rather than those who take lightness away. I do, and it works.

Feel it…

Be aware of the gradual shift toward feeling light and the wonderful effect it has on your body and your mind. Practice the change of attitude that causes your mind and spirit to lift when you intentionally choose to be positive.

As you move along with your commitment to live lightness every day, imagine yourself as you want to be and as you are becoming:.

* Wisely decisive
* Confident, at ease, peaceful
* Organized in a healthy way
* In a positive frame of mind; happy
* Physically active
* Oriented to the "moment"
* Less serious
* Responsive, attentive to others
* Accepting, nonjudgmental
* More creative
* Comfortable just as you are
* Forward-thinking
* Fearless

"Shoot for the moon. Even if you miss,
you'll land among the stars"
~Brien Littrell

Have you heard the expression "The road to hell is paved with good intentions"? It means that we intend to act but don't. You can waste a whole lifetime intending to act when one or two decisions or steps may have made a profound difference.

Be aware—be very aware! What keeps you from moving in the direction you intend? And conversely, what supports you in moving in that direction? Find out the answers and continue to grow from that knowledge.

"I really want to get in shape, but there are so many projects around the house. I haven't gotten around to signing up for the gym. My friend Nancy gave me the name of a good nutritionist, but I haven't called him yet."
Dorothy, NB, Canada

What's going on here? What should Dorothy be aware of about herself? Once she "gets it" she can deal with it and move on to the path toward a healthier body.

Learn, discover, and grow

There is so much magic inside of you. Take time to learn about it and grow from that knowledge. You cannot help but live light if you become a student of your experiences and of your possibilities. Take each new day and reflect on your discoveries and how they can make a difference in your life.

IMP Wisdom!

Acknowledge the joy, beauty, and magic within you.

Set them free.

Embrace the energy of living lightness!

Living it!

- What do you need to keep your commitment to live lightness?

- How will you get what you need?

- What support would you love to have?

- How will you get it?

Take action!

6 things you can do right away to stay Light:

1. Spend 10 minutes before you get out of bed each morning and reflect on what lightness means for you…. Savor the sight, smell, taste, and sound of it. Feel the energy and calmness.

2. Set your intentions to have a day that embraces lightness.

3. Check in with your lightness buddy.

4. Take a small notebook with you and write about the light-giving events and people of your day.

5. Review your calendar for the week. Any light-zappers on there? If so, right this moment, figure out a way to limit or eliminate them.

6. Slay a dragon!

   You're the best and the lightest!!!!!!!!!!

Take an image with you

I have a friend who kayaks. He is experienced on the water and doesn't hesitate to take his boat out at night. One night after visiting, he launched his tiny boat and started home on a familiar waterway. He said his course was guided by phosphorous fish shining in the deep water. He said, "They light my way!" When I find myself thinking about finding my way through life's issues I often visualize water, the ocean, streams, or rivers. These images, for me, suggest the flow and churn of life. They remind me that light guides me.

175

176

With Gratitude

Martha Keener has been my muse, collaborator, coach, thinking partner and supporter in bringing the vision of lightness to fruition. I am so deeply grateful for all of the gifts Martha brought to this endeavor and for her friendship, love, and devotion to the vision.

Much gratitude goes to those who read the first draft. Thank you to Mary Ann Arcesi, Carolyn Beeley, Marge Kelliher, Judy Leeds, Brenda Milkofsky, and Michelle Peters for your insightful critiques as well as positive support.

Mary Ann, Carolyn and Stephanie have spent time and effort in helping me to think through the branding and marketing of lightness. They inspired, cajoled, and supported me. And we had some lovely playful moments along the way. To my coach Bill Kegg, thank you for being the first to help me identify the concept and for your continued support and idea generation.

For your artistry and expertise, thank you to Janet Kusmierski, Emily Muschinske, Tracy Guth-Spangler and Stephanie Vovas.

Heartfelt thanks to my family and friends for your love and support.

Lightness Notes

Lightness Notes

Lightness Notes

Lightness Notes

182

About the Author

Ann Ernst is a professional coach and the founder of The Foxhill Group, a consulting and coaching firm in Connecticut specializing in organizational and leadership development. Publication of her first book is a defining moment in Ann's life and in her work. Stay connected with Ann to learn more about upcoming events and products based on the lightness principles.

www.thelightnessofbeingyou.com

184